The Kerry Dance

A Play

Tony Rushforth

A Samuel French Acting Edition

SAMUELFRENCH-LONDON.CO.UK
SAMUELFRENCH.COM

Copyright © 2000 by Tony Rushforth
All Rights Reserved

THE KERRY DANCE is fully protected under the copyright laws of the British Commonwealth, including Canada, the United States of America, and all other countries of the Copyright Union. All rights, including professional and amateur stage productions, recitation, lecturing, public reading, motion picture, radio broadcasting, television and the rights of translation into foreign languages are strictly reserved.

ISBN 978-0-573-01814-5

www.samuelfrench-london.co.uk

www.samuelfrench.com

FOR AMATEUR PRODUCTION ENQUIRIES

UNITED KINGDOM AND WORLD EXCLUDING NORTH AMERICA

plays@SamuelFrench-London.co.uk

020 7255 4302/01

Each title is subject to availability from Samuel French, depending upon country of performance.

CAUTION: Professional and amateur producers are hereby warned that THE KERRY DANCE is subject to a licensing fee. Publication of this play does not imply availability for performance. Both amateurs and professionals considering a production are strongly advised to apply to the appropriate agent before starting rehearsals, advertising, or booking a theatre. A licensing fee must be paid whether the title is presented for charity or gain and whether or not admission is charged.

The professional rights in this play are controlled by Samuel French Ltd, 52 Fitzroy Street, London, W1T 5JR.

No one shall make any changes in this title for the purpose of production. No part of this book may be reproduced, stored in a retrieval system, or transmitted in any form, by any means, now known or yet to be invented, including mechanical, electronic, photocopying, recording, videotaping, or otherwise, without the prior written permission of the publisher. No one shall upload this title, or part of this title, to any social media websites.

The right of Tony Rushforth to be identified as author of this work has been asserted by him in accordance with Section 77 of the Copyright, Designs and Patents Act 1988

THE KERRY DANCE

First performed at The Questors Theatre, Ealing, on 25th September, 1999, by the following cast:

Jamie Firth	Glynne Steele
Eily Armitage	Helen Walker
Celia O'Malley	Mari King
Paul Corrigan	Donald Morrison
Sarah Anderson	Kate Allen
Bridget O'Malley	Ffrangcon Whelan
Maureen Firth	Dorothy Boyd-Taylor
Margaret Moorhouse	Mary Davies
Brendan O'Malley	Paul Francis

Directed by **Tony Rushforth**
Set Design by **Tessa Curtis**

CHARACTERS

Maureen Firth, aged 59, widow
Jamie Firth, Maureen's son, aged 30 (in the flashback sequences he is nearly 21)
Bridget O'Malley, Maureen's sister, aged 61
Celia O'Malley, Bridget's daughter-in-law, aged 36
Brendan O'Malley, aged 37, Bridget's son, married to Celia
Eily Armitage, Celia's friend, late 30s
Paul Corrigan, aged 21, old school friend of Jamie
Sarah Anderson, aged 25, Jamie's girlfriend
Margaret Moorhouse, mid 40s, teacher at the convent school and at the WEA

Paul is from Galway, Margaret and Sarah are from the South of England; all the other characters speak with a West Yorkshire accent. (In the flashback sequence in Act II, Scene 2, Bridget and Maureen revert to their County Kerry accent.)

The action of the play takes place in the Meeting Room of a parish hall in the West Riding of Yorkshire

Time: Spring 1961, recalled in 1971

For Mary

ACT I

Scene 1

The Meeting Room behind the stage of the St Joseph's RC Parish Hall in Threshton in the West Riding of Yorkshire

Built in 1930, the Hall is a utilitarian building used for meetings, clubs, dances, whist drives, etc. The Room is in need of decoration. There is an archway UR *which leads to an "offstage" double door;* RC *is the kitchen hatch which has a deep shelf that projects into the Meeting Room;* DR *is the door to the kitchen. When the kitchen door and/or the kitchen hatch sliding doors are open we see the shelves and domestic properties suitable for a small overused kitchen.* UL *is a door which leads to the cellar where properties and costumes are stored. A 6" raised level links the cellar door to the* UR *"offstage" double doors. The windows, looking out on to the car park, are in the fourth wall (indicated by gobos) as is the practical central gas fire*

There are nine undistinguished wooden chairs and one wooden desk chair with arms which is set behind an old desk DL. *Against the wall* L *are some stacked card tables and one upright card table which is near an old upright piano and a stool, with a statue of the Virgin Mary on the piano. There are two rows of clothes hooks: one* DS *of the cellar door and another* DS *of the piano. By the* DL *door to the car park is a notice board which includes a poster for St Patrick's Ball, for Friday, March 17th. There are three large central lights, with faded green metal shades and a separate light above the notice board*

Jamie, aged 30, is in a spotlight, wearing a wet mackintosh and holding a bunch of white roses. It is raining heavily and we hear the piano accompaniment for The Kerry Dance

During Jamie's speech, the Lights slowly come up and the piano accompaniment for The Kerry Dance *gradually fades*

Jamie This Meeting Room is at the back of the stage in our Parish Hall. It was built between the wars on a low budget and it was always in need of decoration. It seems so much smaller than I remember; I've been to whist drives here with the card tables spilling out on to the stage, just as they did for refreshments at St Patrick's Ball. In those days the big bands drew in the crowd with their faint echo of Geraldo, and Auntie Bridget was always asked to sing *The Kerry Dance*—she wouldn't use the microphone. (*He places the bunch of roses on the piano where they remain until the end of the play*) Youth Club was in here and the Scouts. The Catholic Women's League ran Bring and Buy Sales, and always and for everything tea was brewed in the kitchen. You can still smell it. Then there was the annual Parish Concert which transformed this room into a Dressing Room and the Parish Hall, for me, briefly became a real theatre. It was magic. It was wonderful. From time to time, when I least expect it, memories of this place come flooding into my mind of family and friends who, in this very room, helped to shape my life, helped to give it some kind of meaning. (*He crosses to the window*)

The general Lighting starts to fade

It's always raining in Threshton—or so it seems. It's because of the moors. And then there's Kilstone Crag which, even on a sunny day, casts a foreboding shadow over the place, shaped like an eagle, keeping a beady and a watchful eye on us all. I haven't been here for ten years—the year that we did *Riders to the Sea*.

Jamie turns, moves right, and sees Bridget, Sarah, and Celia as Maurya, Norah, and Cathleen in 1904 peasant costumes for the final moment of Riders to the Sea. *They are* UC *on the raised area. Norah is kneeling*

We can hear Britten's Moonlight *from* Sea Interludes *to* Peter Grimes. *The three characters from* Riders to the Sea *are atmospherically lit—everything else is in darkness*

Bridget (*as Maurya*) The end is come. May Almighty God have mercy on Bartley's soul, and on Michael's soul and may he have mercy on my soul Norah. (*She places her arm round the kneeling Norah. To Cathleen*) What more can we want than that? No man still can be living for ever and we must be satisfied. (*She makes the sign of the cross*)

Cathleen kneels. Tableau—the Lights fade with the music. We hear applause for eight seconds in the Black-out

Immediately, Eily enters from the car park door, carrying a shopping bag. She is an attractive and vital woman in her late 30s

Eily switches on the DS *lights, then crosses to the* US *wall and switches on the*

Act I, Scene 1

US *lights. She then takes out matches from her shopping bag and lights the gas fire. In the bag is her prompt copy for* Riders to the Sea *and a clip file with details of the Parish Concert*

> *Celia enters from the stage door, holding a tin of biscuits. She is 36 years old, not as attractive as Eily. She takes Eily by surprise*

Celia I thought you'd be here.

Eily I didn't expect you so early.

Celia I'm going up to confession, that's why I've slipped in now (*she indicates the tin*)—tin of biscuits for the refreshments. (*She puts the tin on the hatch shelf*)

Eily Is Bridget at Novena?

Celia She's going over later. She didn't get back from Leeds Infirmary till late.

Eily How is she?

Celia He's given her a special prescription. I think she's a bit embarrassed, so don't say anything—not even to Maureen; promise? (*In a quiet tone*) Waterworks.

Eily Oh. Course I won't. Is she all right?

Celia She seems all right but she looks tired. Mind you, we're that busy I'm not surprised. I shouldn't have taken on this part, I just don't seem to have the energy. It's going to mean a lot of rehearsals.

Eily It'll do you good. Take you out of yourself. You told me you enjoyed being in the plays.

Celia They were just comic sketches. You missed nothing! No, this one is much more demanding. I only hope I don't let the side down, especially Bridget, I'm glad she got the part.

Eily The accent was terrific.

Celia Normally she only slips into it when she talks about the old days in Kerry. She's lived here for over forty years. There were three of them, Bridget, Maureen and Dorothy—she died last year.

Eily Bridget missed her vocation. Imagine what she's going to be like at the concert.

Celia That's how I met Brendan. It was my first concert.

Eily You were lucky there and having Bridget as a mother-in-law.

Celia She's wonderful, doesn't interfere, what do they say? Keeps her counsel. (*She pauses*) I think Brendan takes me for granted.

Eily Course he doesn't.

Celia It's not just that. I want to put things right.

Eily What things?

Celia (*after a pause*) At my age I can't wait any longer if I'm to have a baby.

Eily See the doctor.

Celia I did. I've been having tests—but no sign. I think it's a punishment because … because I insisted that we put off having kids. Because of the Guest House.

Pause

And, I haven't been able to confess it. I told Brendan it was my responsibility, not his. (*She meets Eily's eyes*)

Eily You mean you…?

Celia Yes. I prayed about it but it didn't seem to help. I've had no peace of mind. Oh God, Father Kerrigan isn't an easy priest.

Eily You are being very hard on yourself, Celia. You did what you thought was best. You'll cope with Father Kerrigan. As far as sex is concerned, it's all straight out of the seminary manual!

Celia Don't make it worse.

Eily Sorry, love. But why go tonight? Put it off until the weekend when you've more time.

Celia No, I've put it off long enough and tomorrow's my birthday—so I can really make a fresh start and go to Communion.

Eily (*holding Celia's arms*) You'll be all right. Get it over with, put it all behind you. And don't get scruples. And don't worry, he's heard it all before.

Celia Thanks, Eily. I want to put Brendan at ease, it hasn't been easy for him.

Eily Course you do.

Pause

Cheer up. Marriage can't always be like courting. I'm a fine one to talk. Spinster of this parish!

Celia Well, there's always Charlie Mitchell, he's been a widower for three years.

Eily No, thank you. I don't want to help him with Scouts and I certainly don't want to become the Scoutmistress!

Celia laughs

That's better. There's a good film on at the Regal this week with Peter Sellers, they say it's a real laugh. Why don't we go on Friday night?

Celia I'll see if Brendan's free.

Eily Perhaps we could make a night of it and afterwards have supper at Wendy's Cafe.

Celia You're on. Having a threesome will help, act as a…

Eily Catalyst? Well, I'll do my best.

Celia And don't forget. Your bike's still in our shed.
Eily Sorry, love. I'll mend the puncture tomorrow. (*She goes back to the chairs*) It's getting late, if you want to be first in the queue you'd better get a move on. Miss Moorhouse hopes to start the rehearsal by eight twenty. She's got a parents' evening.
Celia All right, I'll be off.
Eily It will be over in a flash. Don't worry, love.
Celia I'll say my penance later. I'll be back in time.
Eily Off you go—see you soon.

Celia nods and smiles, tears in her eyes as she goes out through the car park door

Eily looks after her, turns away and sighs. She completes placing six chairs in an informal semi-circle

Eily looks at her watch, turns on the cellar light and exits to the cellar

Paul and Jamie enter from the stage door. Jamie is taller than Paul, Paul is more "Latin" and more handsome. They both have the exuberance and the promise of youth which, for them, is difficult to contain. Paul is carrying a cardboard box and Jamie a record player and an LP record

Paul Your mother wouldn't like you slipping out before the end.
Jamie I thought we'd give Eily a hand. (*He smiles wryly*)
Paul Oh yes. (*He looks round the room*) It looks as though she doesn't need it.

Jamie puts the record player and the record on the card table. Paul puts his box on a chair US

Jamie Trust Eily to be ready.
Paul (*passing a brochure to Jamie*) Well? What do you think? I've phoned them and they have two places. (*He looks over Jamie's shoulder at the brochure*) Just look at that view over the lake. We could get the train to Carnforth and then bus it to Keswick.
Jamie Paul, I'd love to go, but it will be the weekend (*quietly*) after my London trip.
Paul If you've got the courage to do that, you can certainly fit in a weekend Art Course. They even offer an option on Set Design, but I think I'll opt for Landscape Painting.
Jamie In the Lakes? All that rain.
Paul Who cares? You'll come?
Jamie No. I'm sorry. I'd better stay at home and face the music—as much as I'd like to escape. Why don't you take Lizzie?

Paul It's finished. That's if it ever started. Put it this way: I made a mistake.
Jamie I'm sorry.
Paul No need to be.
Jamie Is she upset about it?
Paul Not particularly. Hardly a boost to my male ego. (*He shrugs his shoulders*) Anyway, I wanted to get away—it wasn't ... working out.
Jamie It's also about time I considered Sarah.
Paul Well, this course is hardly her cup of tea. They haven't got an option in floral decoration.
Jamie Don't be spiteful. What have you got against her anyway?
Paul She's not your type. And she's playing every game in the book.
Jamie Game?
Paul Grow up. Sometimes you're so naïve.

Eily enters from the cellar, carrying a bag, and turns out the cellar light

Eily Hallo, lads.
Jamie What have you been doing?
Eily Looking at the mess in the cellar. It needs a right good clean 'cos we'll need it as a workshop for this play. (*Meaningfully*) Won't we, Paul?
Paul (*sending her up*) I'm relying upon your "technical expertise".
Eily Come on, let's see the model.

The car park door opens and Sarah enters. She is 25 years of age and very attractive. She speaks without a Yorkshire accent

Hallo Sarah.
Sarah Hallo. (*To Jamie and Paul*) Hallo everyone.

Paul picks up the cardboard box

Paul Hi!
Jamie You are just in time to see the unveiling of Paul's set design.

Paul stands on one of the chairs and takes up a theatrical position with the box, hums the first few bars of the Twentieth Century Fox logo music

Paul (*with an American accent*) Riders to the Sea! (*He starts to take the model out of the box*) It got Miss Moorhouse's seal of approval and she's the producer. (*To Eily*) You are only the Stage Manager. (*He goes to put the model on the desk*)
Eily I'd watch it if I were you.

They gather round the model

Act I, Scene 1 7

Jamie It's not a box set. It's beautiful.
Paul I wanted to get away from all that and try something different. (*He puts his arm round Jamie's shoulder, drawing him in to look closely at the model*) The only solid part is the open fireplace. The rest of the room is suggested by the fishing nets and the painted flagstone floor.
Eily It gives a real feeling for the sea.
Jamie Yes—I love the different tones of green; "dark and menacing". (*He tries to draw Sarah in*) What do you think, Sarah?
Sarah You're very clever, Paul.
Eily First question. Where are we going to get the fishing nets?
Paul Ever looked at the grammar school cricket nets? They'd do. Lizzie's dad knows the groundsman, they won't need them until May.
Sarah But Lizzie hasn't got a part. She was furious when Miss Moorhouse gave it to me.
Eily Well, Paul, it's up to you to persuade her to be in the crowd scene. Miss Moorhouse needs five more.
Paul How can I persuade her?
Sarah You've been taking her to the pictures nearly every Saturday since Christmas.
Paul That stopped...

Sarah gives him an enquiring glance

...for Lent. I haven't seen much of her lately. I don't think she liked me going to night school.
Sarah What art classes are you following?
Paul Still Life and Life Class.
Eily She didn't want you drawing those naked women!
Sarah Thought the temptation might be too strong?
Paul No. (*He has over-reacted*) She didn't say exactly what—just that it embarrassed her—telling her friends.
Eily Well—if she saw the model she'd be proud of you.
Paul Thanks, Eily. Miss Moorhouse was really helpful and yet she was happy to latch on to my ideas.
Eily What's she like? As a person? I don't really know her apart from the audition evening when I was impressed.
Sarah (*cynically*) Ask Jamie—he thinks she's wonderful.
Jamie Don't be ridiculous. (*To Eily*) She started this WEA class in Dramatic Literature and it's great. I didn't know anything about Ibsen or Chekhov. She makes the plays live. She makes you understand the characters and what (*he searches for the phrase*) motivates them into action.
Sarah See what I mean?
Eily I'm not questioning her knowledge of theatre, although I think she might be a bit high-falutin for us.

Sarah Exactly.
Paul It was Father Kerrigan's idea.
Eily You mean choosing Synge.
Paul Yes, (*he imitates Father Kerrigan*) "Ireland forever".
Jamie Well, to do something serious came from Father Kerrigan and Bridget introduced him to Miss Moorhouse.
Paul Who recommended *Riders to the Sea*.
Jamie Ideal for the Drama Festival.
Paul We've never entered the Festival before: "St Joseph's Dramatic Society".
Jamie We've never been called that before.
Sarah Maybe Miss Moorhouse has ideas above her station?
Jamie Maybe she'd like to improve our standard.
Paul She's a lovely person, Sarah. I really enjoyed discussing the play with her—you'll like her.
Jamie Father Kerrigan liked the idea of the festival. St Joseph's competing with other groups.
Eily Other denominations? (*She smiles, looks at her watch*) It's nearly time—come along, Paul. I've got the masking tape and the measurer. (*She takes them out of the bag that she brought from the cellar*) Ground plan?

Paul takes it out of the cardboard box

We've just time to mark out the set and move all the flats.

Paul and Eily exit by the stage door

Sarah What's the record player for?
Jamie The incidental music for the play. Margaret, (*he corrects himself*) Miss Moorhouse, thought it would give some atmosphere at the first reading.
Sarah So it's "Margaret" now.
Jamie She doesn't like the formality of "Miss".
Sarah Well, Bridget always calls her Miss Moorhouse and she's been staying there since the New Year.
Jamie That's only because Bridget, hard though it is, prefers to keep a certain distance from the paying guests. What's the matter? You seem to be getting at "Miss Moorhouse" (*he emphasizes the name*) all the time. She likes you—she cast you in the play instead of Lizzie. In fact she invited you to go with us to Leeds next week to see the *The Cherry Orchard*. It's a wonderful play. It's about "the old order changeth", you know, "giving place to the new".
Sarah Well, I don't want to go—it's not my sort of thing. (*In a mocking tone*) "The old order changeth"... You quote her all the time. You did it just now

with Paul and Eily when talking about the course. Have you lost your own voice?

Jamie (*hurt*) I don't think so. You must try to understand that after two years at Firth's, Margaret has opened up new horizons for me. Studying plays with her has helped me to become—more confident about what I think—about what is good and what is bad in literature and why. It's such an escape from the slog of City and Guilds.

Sarah I'm amazed your mother let you go.

Jamie Bridget had to plead with her. The classes have made the year bearable.

Sarah Bearable? But what about me? Don't I count?

Jamie Of course you do.

Sarah Well, you've got a funny way of showing it. I bet you don't talk about me to anyone else, in the same way that you talk about "Margaret". I think you've got a crush on teacher.

Jamie Now you're being petty.

Sarah I've almost got to make an appointment to see you nowadays.

Jamie She's helping me, with some work.

Sarah What kind of work?

Jamie I can't tell you, not yet.

Sarah I see, secrets. Is that what you were sharing with her in *The Rose and Crown*?

Jamie looks at her

Edna Tosney from your piece room saw you together, "having an intimate chat", she said.

Jamie It's good to talk over what we've been covering in the class, in a more relaxed atmosphere.

Sarah But the others didn't go over to the pub.

Jamie No. They had things to do.

Sarah Who issued the invitation?

Jamie Margaret did, the first time.

Sarah Then you returned the compliment?

Jamie Exactly.

Sarah How cosy. Then there were the pictures in Bradford last week, the theatre in Leeds next week. It's getting quite difficult to fit me in, isn't it?

Jamie I'm sorry if I've been neglecting you but there is a reason which I can't yet explain.

Sarah Why?

Jamie I want to tell you when I know it's all a certainty.

Sarah Can you imagine how hurtful that is to me? That, in some way, I can't be trusted with your secrets and yet Miss Moorhouse can.

Pause

I think you're trying to avoid me because of the other night.
Jamie When we were babysitting?
Sarah Yes.
Jamie I'm sorry.

Pause

I couldn't...
Sarah You made me feel ... cheap, not wanting to...
Jamie You knew I'd just been on the men's retreat.
Sarah Men's retreat! Jamie, it's time you grew up and behaved like a man. I reach out to you all the time but you seem unable to return it. I don't know where I stand. We've been going out for six months, but you don't seem to be able to commit yourself. The relief manager has asked me out twice to dinner at The Midland. Maybe I should have gone with him.
Jamie Trying to get your own back and make me jealous? You know I can't afford The Midland.
Sarah Well, it's nice to know that someone is really interested in me.

Pause

Don't you understand? I want you to be attracted to me ... as a woman.
Jamie I am, Sarah. You'll have to help me. I'm really sorry. Forgive me?

Pause

Can I walk you home tonight and we'll talk?
Sarah (*after a pause*) I don't know. I'll think about it.
Jamie (*taking her hand*) Please?
Sarah (*breaking away*) I said I'll think about it.

Pause

Oh, put on the record—let's hear Margaret's music.
Jamie No. I don't want to steal her thunder. It's wonderful music. (*He looks at the record sleeve*) *Sea Interludes* from Britten's *Peter Grimes*. It fits the mood of the play. "Builds climactically to the storm".

Bridget and Maureen enter from the stage door. Bridget is 61 years of age and smartly dressed, a woman of considerable vitality. Her sister Maureen is 59 years of age; you can see she has been pretty, but she lacks Bridget's

Act I, Scene 1

flair for dress and sense of humour and is a less endearing woman; she is carrying a handbag and a shopping bag containing milk, tea, and sugar

Sarah (*mocking*) "I don't want to steal her thunder". (*Critically and cold*) "Builds climactically". Quotation time again?
Jamie (*raising his voice*) What if it is? She's worth quoting.
Sarah That's obvious. But you've no idea how stupid you sound. It's about time you grew up and behaved like a man.

Jamie looks at her with animosity, she holds his glance contemptuously

Bridget Are we interrupting anything?
Sarah You'd better ask Jamie.

Sarah goes out through the stage door

Bridget What an atmosphere! "Fasten your seat belts—we're in for a bumpy ride".

She laughs, it breaks the mood

Do you remember when we saw that Bette Davis film?

Jamie nods

Maureen I'll see to the tea. (*She crosses to the kitchen*) I've brought it all with me.
Bridget Celia's left the biscuits. (*She indicates the hatch shelf*) You were barely eleven. I'd read it in the *Telegraph* and *Argus*. "Bette Davis makes her first British film in the Dales." Mr Mitchell at the Regal said "Miss Davis will be visiting my cinema one evening next week".
Maureen (*critically*) Storytime.

Maureen exits to the kitchen, turning on the kitchen light, and closes the door—from time to time we hear her working in there

Bridget (*calling after Maureen*) Oh—but it's a lovely story. (*To Jamie*) We sat behind Bette Davis...
Jamie ...watching Bette Davis...
Bridget ⎫
Jamie ⎭ (*together*) ... watching *All About Eve*.

They laugh

Jamie I can't tell you how excited I was. And you took me up to Gargrave late at night to watch them shooting a scene at the railway station.

Bridget I know, and your mother was furious when she found out. All we saw were the arc lights, the rain machine, as if they needed it, and some posh caravans, but it didn't seem to matter.

Jamie For me it might have been Pinewood Studios.

Bridget You were always stage struck. Making toy theatres in your front room and inviting me in to watch the show. You even handed out programmes, but your mother (*she laughs*) couldn't always be bothered, too busy getting our tea ready.

Jamie Or off to the Legion of Mary.

Bridget You know I always wanted to go on the stage—be a real professional. I was invited to join the Catholic Players at the Alhambra in Bradford. Hanson's agent saw me and offered me a tour in the chorus...

Jamie (*smiling, quietly*) *The Chocolate Soldier.*

Bridget A six months contract. I had to turn it down.

Jamie Yes, you told me (*he smiles*) once or twice! But I like that story.

Bridget What you don't know is that me father went mad. It was hell and damnation for a girl in them days to go into the theatre and especially in the chorus, all those stage door Johnnies. Also, I was engaged to your Uncle Bill, the wedding was all planned. I've no real regrets, but sometimes, like tonight, because of you, (*she pauses*) I wonder what would have happened if I'd taken up Hanson's offer? (*She glances at the shutter and speaks quietly*) And what about you? When's the audition?

Jamie Two weeks on Saturday.

Bridget A nephew of mine trying for RADA. I'm that excited. Are you ready for it?

Jamie Nearly. Miss Moorhouse has given me a lot of help with the speeches.

Bridget I'm praying for you, love. And Sarah doesn't know.

Jamie That's part of the trouble—hence the scene when you arrived. Paul knows. Not a word—to anyone.

Bridget Course not. Jamie?

Jamie What?

Bridget I know it's none of my business—and Sarah's a nice enough lass, but my advice, love, would be not to get trapped.

Jamie Trapped?

Bridget To put it bluntly, I think Sarah's a bit keen. You've got your whole life in front of you, so take plenty of time—plenty of time.

Jamie Yes. I want to be certain... I do like Sarah but she doesn't give me enough room.

Bridget Please God, you'll soon have a lot of room. But this is going to be a big shock for your mother. So remember, be strong. Have courage—you're going to need a lot. Don't let the rest of your life be tinged with "what might have been". (*She holds his hands firmly and looks into his eyes*)

Act I, Scene 1 13

The hatch with sliding doors is opened from the inside of the kitchen by Maureen

Maureen Have you two enjoyed going down memory lane?
Jamie Yes, we have.

Bridget winks at Jamie. Maureen has prepared the tea things and the biscuits—they are neatly arranged on a tray on the inside counter that is level with the hatch shelf. She closes the kitchen door and comes into the Meeting Room

Maureen I had to clear up a lot of stuff. Wait till I see Charlie Mitchell—Scouts were in here last night. You can't swing a cat—you have to keep it tidy. And there's no strength in that gas jet, it needs servicing.
Bridget Get Eily to tell Father Kerrigan—he listens to her.

Paul enters by the stage door

Paul Where have you been? I need help stacking the flats.
Jamie Sorry, I got sidetracked.

Jamie exits with Paul

Maureen (*with her handbag*) I've brought you Tony's letter. (*She takes it out*) The Bishop's going to move him in September to Rome—to the Beda College. Three years there, then, please God, ordination. It will be here at St Joseph's—just imagine, the whole parish will turn out for that.

They settle DS in front of the gas fire

Bridget That's good news, to study in Rome. A late vocation is a wonderful thing. At least by then you should know what you want and what you are giving up.
Maureen (*interrupting*) Tony's only thirty, some of them are in their forties.
Bridget I'm sure he'll persevere—if it's what he really wants.
Maureen Persevere? Of course he will. He spent two years praying and thinking about it before he went. He knew what the world had to offer, Bridget, and he turned his back on it in order to help others—to give his life to the church. (*She gives Bridget the letter*) When you've read it let me have it back.
Bridget (*tactfully*) I don't know whether you realize it but these past two years with Tony at the seminary have put an awful strain on Jamie.
Maureen Strain?

Bridget He's been forced to make a go of it on his own. Uncle or no Uncle, Ernest Firth can be a difficult man and well you know it.
Maureen You don't have to tell me that.
Bridget (*carefully*) Jamie's not happy at Firth's.
Maureen Has he talked to you about this?
Bridget (*evasively*) Not in so many words—but I can sense it.
Maureen Happy or unhappy, Bridget—work is work and well you know it. One day the mill will be his. It's doing well now—the orders are coming in. Not like my time in the depression, some weeks they dropped us down to two looms.
Bridget (*pointedly*) You always loathed it. Remember you had an escape route. You got out; you married the boss's son. Remember what Katie Vaughan said before she knew you were going out with Joe? "The trouble with you, Maureen," she said, "is that cloth caps aren't good enough and top hats won't come". Well, you got your top hat. (*She laughs*)
Maureen I don't know about top hat. At first we had to manage on very little.
Bridget That's all changed, thank God.
Maureen Since Joe's death, Ernest Firth has kept me on a tight pension.
Bridget You've no mortgage and you'll get the old age pension.
Maureen Don't wish my time away.
Bridget I don't, Maureen, but we all have to make plans for the future. (*She rises and puts the letter in her handbag*)
Maureen You're all right. The Guest House is doing well. Your Brendan and Celia work hard and please God there will be a grandchild.
Bridget I doubt it. Celia's thirty-six tomorrow—they've been married five years. No, I think that's something I'll have to accept. (*She crosses to the* US *clothes hooks to hang up her coat*)
Maureen I feel for her. It must be a terrible cross to be barren.

Bridget turns to face Maureen

Bridget That's an old-fashioned word.
Maureen It's out of the Bible.
Bridget Yes, I know. Nevertheless, there's something very harsh about it. I don't think Celia would like you using it, Maureen. Not many people do nowadays.
Maureen You mean I'm old-fashioned?
Bridget No—just a bit insensitive.
Maureen (*rising*) You, talk to me, about being insensitive. You're a fine one.
Bridget I don't like your tone, Maureen, and I don't want to fall out. They'll all be here soon so we won't say anything more about it, except that Celia's a grand lass, she really loves my Brendan, he's very fortunate.
Maureen I don't doubt it. I like Celia.

Pause

Pity she's a bit highly-strung.

Maureen goes into the kitchen to brew the tea and Bridget crosses to the hatch

Bridget She works too hard, and Brendan's often a bit sharp with her. I don't like to interfere.
Maureen I'm the same.

Pause

What about Sarah and Jamie when we came in? It won't last.
Bridget You mean you hope it won't. She's a nice enough lass, but I don't think Jamie's ready to settle down. He's too young.
Maureen Course he is. She fancies herself. They moved here from Leicester. Her mother has migraines and she's always ailing.
Bridget I don't know the family.
Maureen Sarah's put out because of the time he spends with Miss Moorhouse and I can understand that. Miss Moorhouse should have more sense. If it isn't one outing it's another. Last week it was a French picture in Bradford, French if you please. Well *you* know, he calls round to see her at your place often enough. I don't like it, Bridget.
Bridget They talk; in the lounge or sometimes I'll make a coffee and they'll have it in the kitchen with me. For Jamie she's something different. She can tell him about the London theatre; the plays, the actors, the companies. His eyes are wide open, soaking it all in. It's lovely to see his enthusiasm.
Maureen But you're not always there.

Eily and Sarah enter by the stage door

Eily We've finished.
Bridget We ought to get started. Tea's ready.
Eily (*shouting; off*) Tea's up.
Paul (*off*) We're coming.

Maureen enters from the kitchen, pushing a trolley with a large tea pot, milk jug and sugar basin

Maureen Miss Moorhouse is late.

We hear the sound of cars leaving the car park

Sarah (*crossing to the trolley*) Can I give you a hand, Mrs Firth?
Maureen Thanks. You can put milk in the cups.
Eily Car park is busy tonight.
Maureen Confessions after Novena. (*To Sarah*) And you weren't at Novena.
Sarah I had to do the ironing. Mother wasn't feeling too good, one of her migraines.
Maureen Oh, I'm sorry. (*She catches Bridget's eye*)

Paul and Jamie enter from the stage door

During the following lines, Maureen pours out the tea at the trolley and Bridget and Sarah pass round the tea and biscuits

Jamie It's great to see the stage cleared, no clutter, just space.
Paul It will seem even better when we've painted the backcloth white and got rid of that woodland glade.
Sarah What do you want to do that for?
Paul It's chocolate box stuff.

With Jamie and Eily, Paul consults the model and puts a piece of white paper against the back of the model

I could light the backcloth as if it were the night sky—and project clouds on it!
Sarah (*cutting through their enthusiasm*) These biscuits are lovely, Mrs Firth.
Eily (*to Paul*) That would be a bit fanciful—even distracting.

Eily and Paul consult the model, Jamie plugs in the record player and puts the LP on the turntable

Maureen They're not mine. Mrs O'Malley made them.
Bridget I'm glad you like them. They're easy to make.
Sarah I'll bring some on Friday.
Maureen Thanks, love, but bought ones wouldn't do for me—I never touch them.
Paul (*to Eily*) Perhaps just to have that effect at the beginning and at the end.
Eily (*to Paul and Jamie*) You'll have to check with Charlie Mitchell, he's always done the lighting and I don't want him upset.

Celia enters by the car park door and has heard Eily's words

Celia No. We don't want Charlie Mitchell upset, do we?

Act I, Scene 1

Eily Watch it.

The boys laugh

> You seem more like your old self.
> **Celia** Yes, thanks. I feel a lot better.
> **Eily** I'm glad. (*She winks*)

Celia smiles

Celia I'm not late. Miss Moorhouse is just parking her car.

During the following, they move to sit on the chairs; left to right: Maureen, Bridget, Celia, Sarah, Jamie, and Paul. Eily is behind the desk

Bridget (*having noticed the exchange*) Are you all right?

Celia nods

Maureen Tea, Celia?
Celia Thanks, Auntie Maureen. (*To Bridget*) Have you a hanky?
Bridget Yes, love. (*She hands her one from her pocket*)
Celia Got a touch of hay fever.
Bridget It's too early for hay fever. Hope it's not a cold.
Celia No. It's just me eyes. (*She hands Bridget the handkerchief*)
Bridget (*concerned*) No, you keep it. Have your tea. (*She passes her the cup from Maureen. To Paul and Jamie*) Help yourselves to biscuits.
Celia (*drinking*) That's lovely.
Maureen Nothing like a good cup of tea to warm you.
Eily (*to everyone*) Have you all got your books?
Sarah They were very expensive.
Jamie Well, you got twenty-four one act plays—all together, quite a bargain.
Sarah But I only needed *Riders to the Sea*.

Margaret comes in from the car park door carrying a briefcase. She's an attractive woman in her mid 40s

Paul and Jamie rise

Margaret Sorry, everyone, the parents' meeting ran over time. (*To Paul and Jamie*) Do sit down—no need for any ceremony. (*She smiles at Jamie and takes off her coat*) Impossible organisation, Reverend Mother told them all to come at six o'clock instead of staggering them in groups. You should have seen the queue!

Eily takes her coat

Thanks!
Maureen Tea, Miss Moorhouse?
Margaret Thanks. I'm dying for a cup—all that talking. (*She sits behind the desk and takes her copy of* Riders to the Sea *out of her briefcase*)
Maureen Sugar?
Margaret No, thanks.

Maureen passes the tea to Margaret with a biscuit on the saucer

Eily, any news of the programme?
Eily (*consulting her clip-file*) I've seen Father Kerrigan and we're on last before the main interval. We follow the quartets—excerpts from the Operatics ending with *Regular Royal Queen*.
Bridget *The Gondoliers*.
Eily If an encore is needed they'll turn to a selection from *Merrie England*.
Bridget They'll have Winnie Bickerton solo. (*To Margaret*) Lovely contralto, some say she's as good as Kathleen Ferrier. Real style. *Oh, Peaceful England*. Edward German. I've been in it.
Margaret You seem to know their repertoire.
Paul You should be on *Twenty Questions*.
Bridget Get away with you!
Paul I mean it. You're terrific.
Bridget I thought we'd be top of the bill and not just pushed in before the interval.
Eily He wants the Children of Mary Lourdes tableau to be the grand finale with the hymns.
Paul Oh, not again. It takes them twenty minutes to set it all up. All that papier mâché.
Jamie And the stained glass window!

Paul and Jamie smirk audibly

Maureen (*seeing them*) That's enough from you two.
Eily Arthur Rushton's going to compère the whole evening, make jokes, introduce each item.
Bridget Yes, we know the format, Eily, *we've* heard them all before. You haven't! Oh dear. (*She smiles*)
Margaret I hope you'll agree that our play doesn't really need an introduction—I don't want it to get off on the wrong footing.
Bridget I agree. This is not Palace of Varieties. Eily, put it right with Arthur, he'll understand. (*To Margaret*) You have to be so careful, (*she laughs*) you know what I mean?

Act I, Scene 1

Margaret Yes, I do. I don't want to upset the man.

Brendan enters from the stage door. He is 37 years of age, heavily built, with a cheerful disposition, but there is some tension between him and Celia

Brendan Upset which man?
Eily Only Arthur Rushton.
Brendan Impossible. (*He smirks*) Thick-skinned.
Bridget I wouldn't be so sure—he can be very temperamental.
Celia (*to Brendan*) What's brought you over?

Brendan and Celia's eyes meet

Brendan Well, I just wanted to put Miss Moorhouse at ease re the men in the crowd.
Margaret Good news then, Brendan?
Brendan Yes. The Devlin boys called in after Novena. (*To Celia*) They are staying for a minute until I get back—only one room left. (*To Margaret*) And they'll do it.
Margaret Well, thank you, Brendan, that's one problem solved.
Celia (*rising*) Cup of tea, love.
Brendan No, but thanks.

Pause

Are you all right?
Celia I'm fine. Much better.
Brendan I'm glad.

Pause

Must get back, the Devlin boys have got a darts match. By the way, Eily, I've just mended your puncture.
Eily That's terrific. Thanks a million. I'll pick it up after the rehearsal.
Brendan Good luck with the reading, Mother. (*He makes for the exit*)
Eily (*calling after him*) She doesn't need luck.

Brendan laughs and exits

Bridget (*with meaning*) Oh, yes. I'll need all the luck in the world.

Pause

Margaret (*to Eily*) We still need three women. I had a note from Lizzie, she can't be in it.

Jamie catches Paul's eye

Celia Miss Moorhouse, I forgot, things on my mind. I saw Iris. She's the leading light of the Children of Mary and she will make sure we'll be all right...
Margaret That's excellent. (*She smiles*) The production's cast!
Bridget Well, we're all very grateful to them. I was never a Child of Mary. Old Canon Brogan wouldn't let me join. Imagine? I cried at the time.
Eily But why not?
Bridget Thought I'd be a bad influence. He didn't approve of me doing the musical comedy in Bradford. Evidently he once had a curate who produced the Christmas Nativity play and then ran off with the choir girl who played Our Lady.

Jamie and Paul laugh

Paul That's hilarious.
Bridget It wasn't at the time. Terrible scandal. So you see, in the Canon's eyes anything theatrical was...
Paul Suspect?
Bridget That's right—suspect.
Paul Was it in all the papers?
Bridget No. The Bishop kept it very hush-hush.
Maureen Bridget, "charity". It was a long time ago and this isn't the time or place to bring it up. More tea, Miss Moorhouse?
Bridget That's put me in my place.
Margaret No, thanks. It has been lovely for this first meeting to have refreshments and I appreciate the thought, Mrs Firth. However, in future we will be working without a tea break. I'm sure you will agree that it can waste too much time. Hope you won't mind. I don't want to sound too much like "the teacher". (*She smiles*) Believe me, in spite of the hard work, I want rehearsals to be fun.
Bridget Fair enough. We certainly need every available minute to get this play ready.
Margaret And also to be ready for the festival. I've duplicated the rehearsal schedule so you can see when we meet. (*She gives seven sheets to Eily*)

Eily passes the sheets round

Eily Paul's shown me the model and we've marked it out on the stage so it's all ready for Monday's rehearsal. (*She opens her pristine prompt copy*)

Act I, Scene 1

Margaret You don't waste any time.
Celia Eily's stage-managed for the Threshton Players.
Margaret So I gather. (*To Eily*) I'm really glad to have you working on the production. Like me, you're quite new to the parish—we'll have to compare notes.

Eily smiles—pleased

Eily Not a bad idea.
Margaret You can see from the schedule, Mrs Firth, that I won't need you to prompt until April 13th: (*to them all with emphasis*) that is when books are down.

Some consternation

Maureen If it's all the same to you, Miss Moorhouse, I'd like to pop in from time to time, so I can get used to the play. In any case, I'm helping Bridget with the costumes.
Margaret Of course, whenever you like.
Sarah (*checking her schedule*) I've got a Flower Festival in Ilkley on the 25th, Miss Moorhouse. I won't be back until late.

Jamie shows some disapproval and Paul winks at Jamie

Margaret I see. I'll look into that and make some adjustments. All right?

Sarah nods

And another point. My name is Margaret, let's get rid of formalities. OK?

Jamie tries to catch Sarah's eye

I have got some ideas about helping us to find the reality of life in Synge's play. Bridget can give us advice on the accents.
Bridget And Maureen.
Margaret Yes, of course, (*she smiles*) I had forgotten that we have two speech advisors! I'm also trying to get a copy of Flaherty's film *Man of Aran* which should be valuable in helping us to visualise the play's background.
Jamie They showed it at school. It's a terrific documentary.
Sarah I don't like documentaries.
Margaret This is different, Sarah—I'm sure we will all get a lot out of it even though it was filmed in the thirties.

Pause

Now, have you all got your scripts?

They get them from handbags, coat pockets, etc.

Good, I want you to turn to page fifteen so that in a moment you will be ready to start reading the whole play. I talked about the characters at the audition. Tonight I want you to get the feel of the piece in its entirety.

Very gradually the Light encloses Margaret and the actors

But first, I want to establish the mood, to visualise the scene, to let it grow in your mind, in your imagination. I've got some music for you to listen to... (*She gestures to Eily*)

Eily moves to put on the record and sits by the record player

...if it doesn't work for all of you, then use it as an exercise in concentration. (*It must be evident that she is a superb story-teller*) Will you all now close your eyes.

They all do except Sarah

You too, Sarah.

Eily has put on the record and we hear Britten's Moonlight

When the lights slowly come up, we see Maurya's cottage, close to the sea. (*She rests one hand lightly on Bridget's shoulder*) A storm is brewing. You are on an island, off the West Coast of Ireland. The year is 1904. Like a camera, the lights focus on Cathleen, (*she rests one hand lightly on Celia's shoulder*) who is finishing kneading the cake. The cottage door is flung open and Norah enters. (*She rests one hand on Sarah's shoulder*) She carries a small bundle, the remains of the clothing swept up by the sea of Maurya's dead son Michael. Maurya is to discover that she has not only lost Michael but will also lose her one remaining son Bartley. (*She rests both hands lightly on Jamie's shoulder; looks down at him, pauses, claps her hands*)

Eily turns off the music

Open your eyes. Turn to your books.

Act I, Scene 2   23

Pause

And so the play begins.

They look at their scripts

The music swells, Britten's Storm *from* Sea Interludes, *as the Lights around them fade to Black-out—we might hear the first two lines of Synge's play*

SCENE 2

Meeting Room, Saturday afternoon the following week

Outside it is raining. The room is somewhat dishevelled. There are two beer crates partly full of empty bottles on the desk, which is now DS *of the kitchen hatch and some used glasses on the two open card tables surrounded by chairs, and there are a few bottles scattered around the room. A metal dustbin is* US *of the kitchen hatch. Eily's shopping bag and umbrella are on one of the chairs*

After a moment, Eily comes in from the car park door, cheerfully whistling, and starts to stack the glasses, placing them on the kitchen hatch shelf and also puts the bottles into one of the crates

During this action, Brendan enters from the car park door

Brendan You sound happy.
Eily Better than being miserable.
Brendan You're never miserable.

Eily smiles

Thank God, only two crates left.
Eily Yes. But they didn't clear all the glasses and bottles. I'm glad George Wilton won't be in to do his big clean until tonight, otherwise there would be trouble. You know how difficult he can be—"monarch of all he surveys".
Brendan You should have been a writer.
Eily I got School Certificate—distinction in English!
Brendan Well, I didn't!
Eily I should have stayed on to do my high school cert. Poor Dad couldn't afford it and the teachers weren't very inspiring, so I ended up in the Electricity Showroom in Barnsley.

Brendan Your Dad wanted to come back to Threshton?
Eily Yes. I don't regret the move.
Brendan You've done well. Manageress in two years.
Eily Hardly a success story.
Brendan (*seeing an empty bottle and putting it in a crate*) Why has George put off the main clean until tonight?
Eily He had to go to Knaresborough, his granddaughter's baptism.
Brendan I'd love to have kids.
Eily Well, maybe you will one day.
Brendan Nay—I think we've left it too late.
Eily You never know.
Brendan (*after a pause*) I don't want to talk about it.
Eily I'm sorry, love, I didn't mean to…
Brendan It's all right. (*He crosses to the crates*) The van's nearly full, but these will just fit in. I'll have to take the Spring Canal turn pretty slowly. I'm parched—is there a bottle left?
Eily No—they are all dead. But I brought some lemonade. (*She takes a thermos from her shopping bag and two cups and pours out the lemonade and sits on a chair by the* DS *card table*) I put some ice cubes in but they'll have melted by now. It's home-made. (*She passes a cup to Brendan*)
Brendan Thanks. (*He sits next to her*)
Eily You did a wonderful job on the plank. Margaret tried it out last night and it worked beautifully. I stood in for you as "the fourth bearer".
Brendan Jamie didn't fall off?
Eily No—but he's quite a weight, lifting him up off the floor was a bit of a strain, can't afford my back to go.
Brendan Well, don't do it again, Eily. Do you hear? It's not a woman's job, look after yourself.
Eily I don't think a Stage Manager is meant to be looked after, I'm supposed to be looking after everyone else.
Brendan Well, be sensible.
Eily Course I will.
Brendan Cigarette? (*He holds up a packet of ten*)
Eily Thanks. I left mine at home.
Brendan Margaret's full of praise. At breakfast today she said she couldn't do the show without you.
Eily That was good of her. I like Margaret—really respect her.

Brendan lights two cigarettes, passes one to Eily, and puts the matchbox in the ashtray

Brendan I only had one match.
Eily Ta. It's like *Now Voyager*.

Act I, Scene 2   25

Brendan looks at her—not understanding

   The film.
Brendan Oh. Before my time.
Eily Watch it! (*She playfully slaps his leg*) Paul Henreid passes the lit cigarette to Bette Davis and she says the famous line: "Why ask for the moon when we have stars?" Music swells. The End. Not a dry eye in the house.
Brendan Well, I'm no Paul Henreid.
Eily (*with an Austrian accent*) The trouble is you don't have a foreign accent.

They laugh. Pause

Brendan You are far more attractive than Bette Davis.
Eily Thank you.

Pause

Brendan drinks his lemonade. Eily sees the poster for St Patrick's Ball on the notice board, crosses over to it and takes it down. It has started to rain outside

   Well, that's over. (*She puts the poster in the waste bin*)
Brendan Until next year.
Eily Thanks for the duty dance.
Brendan It wasn't a duty. Anyhow, you seemed to be dancing a lot with Charlie Mitchell.
Eily Better than being a wallflower. Celia seemed to enjoy it.
Brendan Yes. She loves dancing. Don't let on to Celia that I've had a cigarette, she'd be furious.
Eily Your secret is safe with me. Catholic hand of honour. (*She holds out her hand*)

They shake hands. After releasing their hands there is an awkward silence

Brendan Haven't heard that expression in years.
Eily We used to say it at school, the solemn promise. And talking of promises you said you'd definitely go on the Pools outing again. Remember Southport last year? We had a great day.
Brendan Yes, smashing. The tea dance in the Floral Hall?

She nods

   They've settled for a Saturday trip this year. Will you be able to get the day off?

Eily You bet. The Electricity Board will have to manage without me. Will Celia be able to go?

Brendan stubs out his cigarette

You haven't finished it.
Brendan I wasn't really enjoying it. No, Celia won't go, she gets sick on the coach.
Eily Of course, I'd forgotten. Poor lass, I'll have to get her a nice present. (*She looks at her watch*)
Brendan Ay.

Pause

Eily It's a quarter to four. We'd better get a move on. (*She stubs out her cigarette*)
Brendan Right, Miss!

Eily picks up a crate

You give that to me. (*He takes it from her*) Look after your back.
Eily I'm enjoying being pampered. (*She puts the flask and the cups back in her shopping bag*)
Brendan (*picking up the second crate and crossing to the car park*) Did you check their address? They've moved from Addingham to Crosshills.
Eily I've got it in my bag. Don't worry. I'll be navigator.

Brendan smiles and exits to the car park

Brendan (*off; calling*) It's raining cats and dogs.
Eily (*at the door*) I've got a brolly. (*She crosses to her shopping bag and then to the car park door with the umbrella*)

She is about to put up the umbrella when Paul enters from the cellar wearing a boiler suit

Paul Eily!
Eily (*turning at the door*) What are you doing here?
Paul I wanted to surprise you, so I came over to tidy up the cellar. (*He turns out the cellar light and closes the door*) Mr Woodhead closed the shop early.
Eily Paul—you're a love. Can't stop to admire your work, we're a bit late with the empties. I'll treat you to a drink—promise. Thanks a million. See you.

Act I, Scene 2

Eily exits through the car park door

Paul crosses over to the door

Paul (*calling off*) I'll hold you to that. (*He closes the door, brushes down his trousers which are dirty*)

Jamie enters from the stage door

Jamie! Got an assignation with Sarah?
Jamie Course I haven't. I just came to see if the room was free to work with Margaret.
Paul For the play?
Jamie No. For the audition.
Paul Well you'd better be out by five 'cos of the Pools meeting, otherwise— (*he dramatizes*) you'll be discovered.
Jamie It won't take more than half an hour.
Paul Cigarette? (*He offers him one*)
Jamie Thanks. (*He looks at his watch*) I've just got time.
Paul So you're back on the weed.
Jamie Afraid so. Put it down to general stress and strain.

Paul lights their cigarettes. They have settled on the desk. They inhale—pause

Paul Remember the secret smokes we had at school—at the back of the bike shed.
Jamie Yes! You the new lad Corrigan. Telling me the facts of life.
Paul I'd forgotten all about that— (*he laughs*) you were shattered.
Jamie I thought you might be better informed. Aged fourteen and the eldest of six.
Paul And I was!
Jamie I still got it all wrong.
Paul What do you mean?
Jamie I had got it into my head that it could only happen if you were married. So when Joyce Brooks in the choir got pregnant I was confused. Remember her? She was eighteen and *single*!
Paul You never checked that up with me.
Jamie I was too embarrassed. Didn't want to own up to my ignorance. Felt I shouldn't be talking about it. You know holy purity and all that. "I've had impure thoughts, Father".
Paul Don't. The nightmare of confession.
Jamie How to say it—how to find the right words in that stuffy box.

Paul In my first year here the Redemptorist Fathers gave the Mission. Remember? It was all hell-fire and damnation!
Jamie And Thursday night was the night they gave the sermon on "purity".
Paul You mean on "impurity"—the only time that they reiterated the word "SEX". I'll never forget how he finished his sermon: (*he rises and uses the table as a pulpit, speaks with a strong Irish accent*) "Before confession this evening I want you to examine your conscience. Have you been impure in thought, word or deed with a member of the opposite sex? Or with a member of the same sex? Or," and I swear he looked me straight in the eye, "WITH YOURSELF!" I went crimson.
Jamie (*after a pause*) Had you?
Paul Course I had. Often. That wonderful release— (*he smiles*) marvellous. Of course, I knew it wasn't something that you asked questions about. It was—private. Although I felt guilty about it, it only concerned me, so how could it be a sin? There was nothing about it in the Bible. Mr Hardacre in Religious Studies hadn't mentioned it. As if Hardacre would! You can imagine my shock and the panic that I'd have to confess it. (*With an Irish accent*) "How many times, my son?" I nearly died. Two years is a long time.

Pause

Surely you did it?
Jamie Well, once or twice.
Paul (*roguishly*) Oh, yes? (*He laughs*)
Jamie But after that sermon I felt I had to confess.
Paul I felt like St Augustine: "Dear God, make me pure, but not just yet!"

They laugh

And nothing's changed. You know that Norman the barber is out of bounds— (*with an Irish accent*) "To be avoided!"
Jamie No, why?
Paul Because he sells french letters...

Jamie looks at him

Condoms!
Jamie (*smiling*) Mother's been sending me to Norman's for years! Where did you hear about it?
Paul John Devlin was at the Men's Guild meeting and Father Kerrigan came over for a chat.
Jamie I don't believe it. (*He stubs out his cigarette*)

Act I, Scene 2   29

Paul (*with a strong Irish accent*) Well, my son, that's the power of the church.

Margaret, wearing a wet mackintosh, enters from the stage door, carrying her handbag and the script for The Cherry Orchard

Margaret Hallo, Paul.
Paul Hallo.
Margaret (*to Jamie*) Sorry I'm a bit late—so much end-of-term marking.
Jamie It is free.
Margaret Are you sure?
Jamie Yes.
Paul (*getting his raincoat from the* DS *clothes hooks and looking at the notice board*) The only booking for today is the Pools Meeting at five.
Margaret That's fine. (*To Jamie*) Right. Thirty minutes hard work on Lopakhin.
Paul Well, I'll leave you to it. Hope it goes well. (*He switches on the* DS *lights*)
Jamie Thanks.
Margaret See you at Monday's rehearsal?
Paul Couldn't keep away. Bye.

Paul exits through the car park door

Margaret Goodbye. (*She starts to take off her mackintosh*) I'd really like to try the speech on the stage for you to work on projection but it's safer in here.

Jamie helps her take off her coat, and hangs it up on the hooks near the car park door

Thanks.

Jamie does the same with his coat

If we get away by four thirty we'll have time to have something to eat. Perhaps at the Kardoma?
Jamie Great. I love the quartet. They remind me of a holiday we had in Scarborough. Mum and Dad liked listening to the Palm Court Orchestra.
Margaret I've never been to Scarborough—"so bracing"! Isn't that what the posters say?
Jamie No, that's Skegness.

They laugh

Margaret It seems damp in here.
Jamie I'll light the gas. The fug from last night doesn't help.
Margaret Yes. It does smell a bit like a saloon bar.
Jamie (*lighting the gas fire*) Father Kerrigan won't have to mind. It's all in a good cause.
Margaret Not a cause that he would support.
Jamie Preparing for my vocation? When I was a boy I couldn't distinguish between vocation and vacation. It led to all sorts of confusion.
Margaret (*smiling*) I can imagine. Did Sarah go to the Ball?
Jamie No.
Margaret Why not?
Jamie There's been a bit of tension recently.
Margaret I've felt it at times at rehearsal.
Jamie Sorry about that.
Margaret What's the problem? Or shouldn't I ask?
Jamie I haven't told her about applying for RADA. She knows I'm hiding something. She ... got into a bit of a state about it.
Margaret I don't understand why you can't tell her.
Jamie I don't think she would like it—my going to London for all that time. Like Mother, she thinks I've got a good career ahead of me at Firth's.

Pause

Margaret Jamie, you know I'm not happy about your mother being kept in the dark.
Jamie I'm dreading telling her. But ironically, if I don't get in, I'll be spared that ordeal.
Margaret What about attending the audition?
Jamie As it's a Saturday I don't need to worry about work. I'll get the early train and go down for the day. I'll think of some excuse.
Margaret It's a mistake to do it in a day. I've got friends in Chiswick where you can stay. So catch the Friday evening train. OK?
Jamie That would be wonderful.
Margaret It's the least I can do.
Jamie You've helped me so much already.
Margaret I've enjoyed it. (*She smiles*)
Jamie (*after a pause*) I don't underestimate what you have done for me.
Margaret It's been my pleasure, Jamie.
Jamie "Thank you" seems so inadequate...
Margaret Please. There's no need to say more. (*To change the subject, she sets up two chairs to represent a chaise-longue*) Did you enjoy the Ball?
Jamie Yes. I came over with Paul. He's a great dancer. You should have seen him do the Twist—fantastic mover. Nearly two hundred people came. It must have made a bomb. You should have come.

Act I, Scene 2   31

Margaret (*smiling*) I think my dancing days are over.
Jamie Nonsense.
Margaret Your Auntie Bridget told me she was on duty with refreshments.
Jamie Auntie Bridget's egg-and-cress sandwiches are quite something. When the big band played *The Kerry Dance* the lights dimmed and I saw her watching from the wings.
Margaret Remembering.
Jamie Yes.
Margaret It's a lovely ballad—"Oh, for one of those hours of gladness, gone alas, like our youth too soon".
Jamie (*interrupting*) You know the words.
Margaret (*smiling*) As a girl I often went to Paddy's Ball in Southampton. I bet they also played *Danny Boy*?
Jamie (*smiling*) You have been here before.
Margaret Oh yes. I have been here before. (*She picks up a faded small shamrock harp which is lying on the floor*) Even the shamrock in the gold harp. (*She laughs*) I've still got one of these.
Jamie From an admirer?
Margaret You could say that. (*After a pause, she puts the shamrock on the table*) This won't do, getting sentimental, we had better get to work. (*She picks up her copy of* The Cherry Orchard *and gestures to the table and dustbin*) This can represent where the guests at the ball gather, the orchestra beyond, and this (*she gestures to the two wooden chairs*) can be where Ranyevskaya is seated. (*She crosses with an empty glass from the kitchen hatch shelf to a card table* DL) This is the drinks table. (*She puts the glass on the table*) You have really got to create the scene. Just imagine her sitting here. How will you relate to her? Do you go down on your knees? Do you speak to her from behind the chaise-longue or from the left or the right?
Jamie Find the spontaneity!
Margaret (*laughing*) Are you sending me up?
Jamie (*laughing*) Of course I'm not.
Margaret (*after a pause*) We've got to concentrate. Look, to help I'll sit in for her. See what happens and then we'll select. Think about the intention that lies behind the phrases. But I'm repeating myself. Bad teaching!
Jamie No. I understand what you mean. I'll give it a go.
Margaret Before we try the whole speech, let's take it from before you go to her. (*She looks at her script*)
Jamie "Villas"?
Margaret No, a bit earlier, "I have bought the property". And remember he was a peasant, so make the Yorkshire accent a bit stronger.

Jamie moves well down L. *Margaret sits on the chair as Madam Ranyevskaya. There is a pause and Jamie picks up the glass*

Jamie I have bought the property where my father and grandfather were slaves, where they weren't even allowed in the kitchen. (*He crosses to the kitchen hatch*) Hey, musicians, play away! Come everyone and see me lay an axe to the orchard!

Maureen and Bridget enter from the stage door and stand surprised, and watch Jamie. Bridget carries a closed, wet umbrella and Maureen a shopping bag with sewing materials

Neither Jamie nor Margaret are aware of their presence

Come and see the trees fall down! Villas! We'll fill the place with villas; our grandsons and our great-grandsons will see a new life here... Music! Strike up some music! (*To Margaret*) Oh, why, why didn't you listen to me? (*He kneels by Margaret and takes her hand*) You can't put the clock back now, my poor dear. Oh, that all this were past and over, that our unhappy life were changed. (*He holds Margaret's hand tightly, pressing it to his face*)

Bridget applauds. Margaret and Jamie turn quickly and see their unexpected audience. They rise and Margaret breaks DL and picks up her handbag. Jamie breaks DR. There is an uncomfortable silence

Bridget Sorry, I just had to clap. Jamie, I could hardly believe it was you. (*To cover the embarrassment*) What's the play called?
Margaret *The Cherry Orchard*—Chekhov.
Bridget I saw one of his plays on TV. This young lad, a writer, killed himself, his mother was an actress.
Margaret *The Seagull.*
Bridget That's right, I remember now, they brought on a dead bird.
Maureen (*putting down her bag on an upstage chair*) When you've both quite finished talking about plays I'd like to know what's going on.

Pause

Margaret is about to speak

Bridget No, Margaret. Jamie, you'd better tell your mother.
Jamie I've got an audition with RADA a week today. Margaret's been helping me with the speeches.
Maureen RADA?
Jamie The Royal Academy of Dramatic Art.
Maureen In Manchester?
Jamie No, Mother, London. It's a full-time course. Two and a half years.

Act I, Scene 2

Maureen Now listen, my lad. I think you've taken leave of your senses.
Margaret (*to Jamie*) Do you want me to go?
Jamie No.
Bridget Please stay. (*To Maureen*) Maureen, he's not taken leave of his senses, he wants to find fulfilment in life. To develop his potential, if you like, *using* the God-given talent, not wasting it. He wants to be a professional actor.
Jamie I think what I eventually want to be is a producer. To be really creative.
Bridget (*to Maureen*) And Jamie *is* creative about theatre. He's been thinking about nothing else for years and well you know it. At school he was the leading light of the Dramatic Society. (*To Margaret*) Played Richard the Second—it was unbelievable. (*To Maureen*) Remember what old Molly Scargill said: "I've seen nothing like it since bloody Henry Irving!" Well, you had to laugh. But I know what she meant. You wouldn't let him join the Threshton Players. You only agreed to him being in the concerts because it was for church. I was the one who made you agree to him going to Margaret's class because I wanted him to have some joy in his life.
Maureen Joy? At the WEA?
Jamie You just don't understand. Everyday when that alarm clock goes I have to force, yes, force myself up, not because I want to go on sleeping, but because I have to face another day at Firth's. When I look at my watch, it's always at least two hours earlier than I think it is—all the time, every day. Then there's what is expected from the boss's nephew, from "*Mr Jamie*". They know in the weaving shed that I'm keeping my eye on them, like being a private detective, so there's no trust. And Uncle Ernest intimidates, he never gives you praise for anything.
Maureen I know Ernest can be difficult but his bark is worse than his bite. Of course, there's the monotonous side, but you like design work, you got the Art Prize at school. The business is starting to take off, they've got some good orders, before long you'll have a good salary and be able to have your own car with money in the bank towards your own house.
Jamie That's not what I want. And about design work—it's a joke. Ginghams and check tablecloths! My heart's not in it. When I listen to the beat of the looms, I think: what if I'm still here when I'm sixty-five?
Margaret Mrs Firth, I had to leave school when I was sixteen, times were hard, my father was ill. I worked on the counter in Boots for six long years and hated it. I went to night school, and then to university. So you see, I can feel for Jamie and identify with his situation.
Maureen How do you think I feel? I came in here to do some work on the costumes, thinking he'd gone off to Leeds and I find him deceiving me. Try to look at it from my point of view.
Margaret We delayed leaving in order to fit in an extra rehearsal. Jamie

didn't intend to deceive you, Mrs Firth. We don't know if he'll be accepted for a place at RADA. The competition will be very keen and (*to Bridget*) Jamie's triumphs in the school play won't count on the day. On the day he will stand or fall according to their assessment of his potential. (*To Jamie*) Sorry, Jamie, it's a bit frightening when I put it like that.

Maureen (*to Margaret*) So you are saying it could be out of his reach?

Margaret I'm saying that I don't know. He has ability, he is talented. I think that if all goes well on the day, he has a reasonable chance.

Pause

Maureen There's an important thing that's been overlooked.

Bridget What?

Maureen Money. If he gets into this place, how he's going to live? All that time living in London. And what about the teachers' fees? They'll be a packet.

Margaret The West Riding give grants nowadays.

Maureen He's already on a grant for the Technical College. (*To Jamie*) You've had your chance—they're not going to give you a second one.

Jamie Well, we will have to wait and see.

Bridget You know whose side I'm on.

Maureen You've made that perfectly clear.

Pause

Margaret Jamie thought that there was no point in upsetting you in case he wasn't offered a place.

Maureen Well, I am upset and I keep thinking of his father. (*To Jamie*) Do you think that all he did for you counts for nothing? Many a time he's said that all the work, all the sacrifice was worth it knowing that Firth's would stay in the family. Now that Tony's at the Seminary, your father's inheritance lies in your hands.

Jamie Inheritance! We've got ninety looms and half of the shed is let off. Any money that's now in the kitty has to be ploughed back into new looms. There will be no expansion. The way you talk you'd think we were *The Crowthers of Bankdam*.

Maureen I'd no idea that you were so resentful.

Jamie Oh yes, I'm resentful. And while we're talking about resentment, you never told me that, before I left school, Mr Ashbourne called you up to his study and said that I should have a career in the theatre.

Maureen looks at Bridget, astonished

Yes, Auntie Bridget told me last night.

Act I, Scene 2   35

Bridget (*to Maureen*) I wanted to build up his confidence. I'm sorry. I weakened.
Jamie (*to Maureen*) So what did you do? You went straight over to see Father Kerrigan.
Maureen To get his advice.
Bridget (*to Maureen*) You know I never approved of that, what does Father Kerrigan know? (*She imitates the priest*) "Sure now he'd be putting his faith at risk. When he's finished his textile studies he can do a bit of amateur dramatics." (*Scornfully*) A bit of amateur dramatics.
Jamie (*vocally he is now on the attack*) Was it fear of putting my faith at risk, Mother? Was it? Did you really fear that if I was in London mixing with "rogues and vagabonds", I might lose my faith? Or was it simply that you knew that Father Kerrigan's advice would exonerate you from any responsibility? He would, like the priest in the confessional, absolve you and your conscience would be clear.
Maureen I did what I thought was best for you.
Jamie Best for me? If you are really being honest, isn't it a question of what is best for you? And what about Tony? You didn't challenge him in terms of duty. Has it ever crossed your mind that the priesthood was the one route that would ensure your blessing? Who knows? It could have been Tony's escape route.
Maureen (*extremely angrily*) How can you belittle Tony's vocation? A vocation is a calling from God. What would you know about it? How dare you insinuate... (*She hits him strongly on the back*)
Jamie (*scornfully, climactically*) Mother, you've got blinkered vision, don't you think it's about time that you faced up to the fact that Tony's vocation is suspect...
Maureen (*overlapping and almost screaming*) I won't listen to you. (*She puts her hands to her ears*)

They are standing close together. Silence

Bridget (*to Jamie*) Jamie, I think you'd better go.

Jamie crosses to his mackintosh. Margaret goes to get hers. Maureen takes her hands from her ears

Maureen I want a word with you, Miss Moorhouse.

Bridget moves a pace to the stage door

Stay, Bridget.
Jamie (*to Margaret*) I'll wait for you at Auntie Bridget's. We should try to get away by five o'clock.

Margaret No. To save time bring the car down. Here are the keys. (*She hands them to him*)

Jamie goes out through the car park door

There is an uncomfortable silence

Maureen (*to Margaret*) You were both behind this conspiracy. (*To Bridget*) I blame you the most. I might have known not to trust you. (*She turns to Margaret with meaning*) Be careful. You're seeing too much of that lad.
Margaret Lad? Jamie will be twenty-one this year.
Maureen People are talking...
Bridget (*to Maureen*) Maureen, that's enough.
Maureen ...about your friendship with Jamie.
Margaret If it wasn't so laughable I would be offended. Yes, I have befriended Jamie at a time when he needed me. He is beginning to ask questions about what philosophers call "the good life". I hope he will find the fulfilment that he's searching for.
Maureen The good life!! In the Depression there was no time to think about the "good life". We just got on with it and thanked God that we had work.
Margaret Mrs Firth, the work ethic can be a negative or positive force in our lives and for Jamie I want it to be a positive one. I sympathise with your fear of losing him. But you'll still be able to see him during his vacations.
Bridget (*to Maureen*) What I've learned, Maureen, is that you can't live your life through your children. They have to shape it for themselves. Look at my David in Melbourne.

Pause

You have to cut the cord, Maureen, that's the hardest lesson that a mother has to learn.
Maureen Has it never occurred to you that you have chosen to live part of your life through Jamie?
Bridget What do you mean?
Maureen You've always had misgivings about not taking up Hanson's offer to go on the stage. David and Brendan had other interests, they weren't "artistic" like you. Oh, yes! you've always made sure you got close to him.
Bridget Of course I was close to him; when Joe was ill he came to live with me, remember?
Maureen (*bitterly*) Oh, yes. I remember. But he was your nephew, *not your son*.
Margaret Mrs Firth, he's torn between a sense of duty to you and his need to break free.

Maureen It's easy for you. You come up here offering him the moon with your fanciful notions, your "philosophers", your ideas about plays, and he gets carried away, he gets smitten. I'd say that he had a crush on you, no more, no less. It's all right for you doing a six month relief job up here. In July you'll be off, without a care in the world, and I'll be left picking up the pieces.

Margaret (*finding it now difficult to maintain her composure*) That's presuming that he won't get into RADA. But if he does, Mrs Firth, it won't be because of me. I haven't offered him the moon. I may have pointed the way and tried to help as far as I could—the rest is up to Jamie. As to Jamie having a crush, if this were so I would consider it a compliment and would know how to deal with it, *if* it were so.

Maureen Be that as it may but after tonight I don't want you to see Jamie again on his own. Do I make myself clear?

The car park door opens—it is Jamie

Jamie I've parked round the corner. I think we should go.
Margaret (*picking up her bag*) I'm ready.

Jamie goes out

Margaret crosses for her coat and goes to the car park door. She turns before going out

(*To Bridget*) Celia gave me a key as I'll be back late. I won't disturb you.

Margaret exits

Bridget She's an upright and honest woman. To speak like that to her, how could you?
Maureen I've heard plenty, Edna Tosney for one. It wouldn't be the first time that a single, middle-aged woman has become "interested" in a young lad. I know my own son. He's not as mature as you think he is. Look how he behaves with Sarah. He doesn't know his own mind.
Bridget Well, one thing's certain, he knows his own mind about RADA and that's something you'll have to accept.
Maureen He's not yet ready to stand on his own two feet away from home. Study theatricals in London? No, he stays here. (*She picks up her bag*)
Bridget Where are you going?
Maureen I'm going over to the presbytery...
Bridget I won't let you do that. Father Kerrigan's done enough damage and Jamie's not in the mood for any priestly advice. I'm telling you that if you go over to the presbytery you'll live to regret the day.

Maureen Will I, indeed? You're a fine one to talk. High and mighty, aren't you? Isn't it about time you came down from your pedestal and told me, face to face, that you had an affair with my Joe.

Pause

I've known since he died. You're in no position to stop me from doing what I have to do. (*Contemptuously*) Me own sister.

Maureen swiftly exits through the stage door

Bridget reaches for a chair, sits and starts to cry as the Lights fade to Blackout

ACT II

Scene 1

The same

Jamie is standing in a spotlight close to the piano

Jamie Mother didn't speak to me for over two weeks. Didn't even ask me about the trip to London. Then the letter came from RADA, offering me a place. I was ecstatic, but for her the letter did not even exist. She didn't go to any rehearsals and so Father Kerrigan had a word with her—comforted by the church, she returned for the final week. It was obviously a big strain, but I suppose in a way she had to do it, to save her face. In spite of everything, I admired this gesture—yet you could still feel the tension between her and Bridget. As for me, although I had apologised—well, to speak to me might be a start. I had to wait for the technical rehearsal before she broke the "magnum silencium". But other problems loomed large on the horizon that evening for both of us. Looking back, what we didn't know was that Auntie Bridget had cancer and would die before the end of the year.

The Light fades on Jamie, and in a moment the Lights come up on the Meeting Room

It is four weeks later, Thursday evening

A costume rail, holding the costumes for Riders to the Sea *is* UL *and two boxes of boots and shoes are on the floor* DS. *A large bin is* UR. *The table and four chairs are now* LC. *A small ground row is on the floor* R—*laid out on newspaper with a pot of dark green paint and a drawing of the ground row is on the kitchen shelf. Paul's portfolio of drawings is leaning on one of the chairs* DL. *There is a poster for the concert on the notice board and a poster for the Drama Festival on the* US *kitchen wall by the hatch*

The only source of light comes from the car park through the windows and from the UR *spill of atmospheric stage lighting as the stage door is apparently open*

Paul, paintbrush in hand, is leaning on the US *wall, watching the technical rehearsal as if from the wings. As Eily has put a speaker on the* UR *wall of the Meeting Room, we can clearly hear the final lines of the play*

Bridget (*off; as Maurya*) The end is come. May Almighty God have mercy on Bartley's soul, and on Michael's soul and may he have mercy on my soul Norah.

Jamie comes in from the DL *door and switches on the* DS *Lights*

Paul sees him

What more can we want than that? No man at all can be living for ever, and we must be satisfied.

Paul closes the offstage door

Margaret (*off*) Fade it out, Charlie, I want to go back to lighting cue twenty-four. Eily standby for sound cue fourteen.

Paul turns the speaker off

Paul I think we can give that a rest.
Jamie I thought the technical would be over by now. (*He puts his coat on the* DS *clothes hook*)
Paul Charlie Mitchell was late, got held up in Burnley. How was the stocktaking?
Jamie Well, my mind wasn't really on it. I could only think of one thing: will the West Riding give me a grant?
Paul You should hear soon. Do you like the tannoy? (*He indicates the back wall*)
Jamie Very sophisticated for St Joseph's.
Paul Eily's idea. The Threshton Players. (*He resumes painting the ground row*)
Jamie What's that for?
Paul The ground row lights for the backcloth were showing.

Jamie looks at the ground row

Margaret's idea.
Jamie I'm impressed with the detail. You haven't told me about your weekend in the Lakes.
Paul You never asked.
Jamie Sorry. I've had a lot on my mind. The strain at home has been awful. Sarah's been very understanding.

Act II, Scene 1

Paul I bet she was—to your face. She's determined to get you. You should have heard her when you cancelled the Youth Hostel Weekend.
Jamie We went out for trips instead. One day we went right up to the top of Kilstone.
Paul (*teasing*) But it's not the same as assignations late at night!
Jamie That's enough. She was very good about it. Brought lovely picnics.
Paul Of course she did! However, what is it you're *not* saying? What Margaret would call "the sub-text"?
Jamie I don't know. I fluctuate.

Pause

I think I'm half in love with her.
Paul You only think? Half in love with her? (*As an innuendo*) Which half?
Jamie Why do you have to reduce everything to sex?
Paul Doesn't have to be that half. But it's a pretty powerful force—difficult to deny it.
Jamie What about the mind and the spirit?
Paul Ideally you want all three.
Jamie I hope you find it—I mean it.
Paul It may take a long time, (*he pauses*) but I'll wait.
Jamie I think you're just feeling vulnerable because it's all finished with Lizzie.
Paul (*guardedly*) That was different. It never would have worked out. It was just something that I felt I ought to try. I wanted to discover myself.
Jamie And did you?
Paul Yes. I think I did. (*He changes the subject; he has completed painting the ground row*) When it's dry we'll try it out on the stage. I'll put some texture on it tomorrow.
Jamie Did you learn a lot?

Paul looks at him

On the weekend course?
Paul Yes, it was terrific. Bob Hurndall who runs the course was great. In his own way he was as inspiring as Margaret. Chap about thirty-eight. Lots of charisma. Lives near Kendal.
Jamie Did you do any work?
Paul Yes. Two landscape paintings. And it didn't rain. We went swimming together.

Jamie looks at him

Indoor pool! Another year at night school and Bob thinks I'll have enough material to apply to Leeds Art School—special entry. He says he'll act as a referee.

Jamie He seems to be going to a lot of trouble to help.

Paul Do I detect some edge in your voice?

Jamie I don't know what you mean. Just pleased for you.

Pause

It looks like your days with Woodhead and Co. are numbered.

Paul Bespoke tailoring has had its day and I don't think they'll survive the change. Oh—to get away.

Jamie Don't remind me. If only I could be certain of a grant.

Paul (*putting his arms round Jamie's shoulder*) You know that I'm willing it to happen. When you get to Drama School you'll be a changed man. You'll discover the real you. I don't think you'll ever want to come back.

Jamie I've got to get there first.

Paul I've got a feeling that you will.

Jamie meets Paul's eyes. After a pause, Paul releases his hold and turns to the finished ground row

I think it will work.

Jamie It's good.

Paul Thanks. (*He cleans his brush*) Bob's going to try and come down and see the play. I showed him the sketches and the model and he liked it. (*He picks up the drawing*) Says I should include it when I apply to Leeds Art School. He's a bit different. Lots of jokes and he's interested in theatre. You'll have a lot in common. (*He crosses* DL *to his portfolio*)

Jamie Is that your art work?

Paul Yes, life class drawings. I had to leave halfway through 'cos of the technical.

Jamie Let's have a look.

Paul They're not very good.

Jamie Don't be modest. Go on.

Paul (*picking up five drawings*) All right, but don't be over-critical. (*He shows him three drawings and stands close to him*) What's the matter?

Jamie I didn't realize they'd be...

Paul In the nude? Not always and male models have a pouch over their willies. You can see. (*Sensing Jamie's embarrassment he laughs and passes him another drawing*) Such a fantastic physique, he was difficult to draw—I'm trying to concentrate on the line to find the movement.

Jamie Well, you have. (*He looks at another drawing*) All men.

Paul No, not always—but I think I'm better with the male models. (*He

Act II, Scene 1   43

    passes another drawing) This one in particular. (*He shows it to Paul*) Isn't he stunning?

Pause

    Well—isn't he?

Pause. Jamie is embarrassed

    You're blushing! I can't believe it. Oh God, I hope I haven't got paint on this. (*He returns the drawings to the portfolio*)

Brendan comes in from the stage door

Brendan Hallo Jamie. (*To Paul*) I've just got here. Missed the early train. Eily wants the ground row in position. She's getting impatient.

Eily enters from the stage door

Eily I am! Come on, you two. Let's get it set. Charlie wants to see if it's going to give sufficient cover. Hallo Jamie. Your mother's downstairs, she told me to let her know as soon as you arrived. Margaret's going to do the ending *again*.

Brendan and Paul exit with the ground row

    (*To Jamie*) Be a love and get rid of all that newspaper.

Eily exits by the stage door

Jamie, left alone, gathers about half of the newspaper together and puts it in the bin

Sarah enters from the stage door

Sarah How are things?
Jamie OK. It's the waiting.
Sarah I know. Brendan's just told me you were here. (*She takes his hands*) I just wanted to see you. I really want you to be able to go to RADA. I know how much it means to you. I've been thinking and I can take some Building Society holidays when it's your term time and come down to London to see you and you'll be up here during your vacations.
Jamie Not necessarily. The grant won't be enough. I'll work whenever I can get a temporary job, so I don't know where I'll get to.

Sarah I've been talking to Dad about it and he says that there might be something going in the office—you know, booking excursions, cashing in the clippies: shift work when the regulars are on holiday.
Jamie That's very good of him.
Sarah Well, it would help—you'd like that?
Jamie We'll see.
Sarah When I was little and Mum said "We'll see", it always meant "no". Don't you want a holiday job in Threshton?
Jamie It didn't mean "no". I'd really like to get a theatre job, however modest. Any professional theatre contact could be useful in the future.
Sarah I can understand that. As long as you're not trying to avoid seeing me.
Jamie If I get to London I've got to make a success of it—I can't risk failure after all this. So I can't take everything on board, not just at the moment. Do you understand?
Sarah Yes, I do. In time, everything's going to be all right. You can teach me about plays.
Jamie Sarah, you mustn't try so hard.
Sarah (*misunderstanding*) I'll be a good listener.

Pause

The technical's taking ages.
Jamie Margaret's a perfectionist.
Sarah Poor Margaret.
Jamie Why "poor"?
Sarah I was just plain jealous. She's a professional woman, it wouldn't cross her mind.
Jamie What?
Sarah The tittle-tattle, Edna Tosney and the others. Stupid.
Jamie I've so much to thank her for.
Sarah When you get your Oscar you can give her a mention!
Jamie I just might.

Pause

We're talking as if I've got the grant.
Sarah You will. (*She crosses her fingers*)
Jamie You do realize that life in the professional theatre isn't always a bed of roses. For the majority, it's a long uphill struggle, waiting for the right person to see you at the right time, in the right part.
Sarah (*teasing*) Quotation time again?
Jamie (*smiling*) Yes it is: but it's true. I don't know why Wakefield's taking so long.

Act II, Scene 1   45

Sarah You were a last-minute application. Be patient.

Pause

>Will you walk me home afterwards?
Jamie Course I will.

She initiates and takes both his hands and draws him close to her—she is about to kiss him

>*Eily enters by the stage door*

Eily Oh—excuse me! Miss Armitage, you are needed on stage.
Sarah Sorry, Eily. I just got...
Eily ...carried away!

Sarah goes out

>(*To Jamie*) Get rid of that paper. And don't forget your mother. (*She switches on the* US *light*)
Maureen (*off*) It's all right, Eily.

Maureen enters from the cellar door and turns out the cellar light. She has a pin cushion and is carrying Sarah's skirt

Eily exits by the stage door

Maureen puts the cushion on the table and starts to take out the pins from the skirt. The following exchange has a curious formality

>So you're back. I've finished Sarah's costume. I had such a lot of trouble with the skirt. Did the stock-taking go all right?
Jamie Yes, fine.
Maureen With so much on your mind it must have been a bit of an effort.
Jamie (*surprised*) Yes, it was.

Pause. Jamie puts the newspaper in the bin

>Thanks for the sandwiches, my favourite.
Maureen And some of my special parkin.
Jamie So I noticed.

Pause. Maureen continues removing pins from the skirt and putting them in her pin cushion. Jamie takes a pace towards Maureen

I'm glad we're speaking.

Maureen (*after a pause*) I got it all out of proportion. It was such a shock—it knocked the stuffing out of me. It made me so angry. Then reason goes out of the window and you say, (*with emphasis*) and do, things that you regret. But I've never seen you like that.

Jamie Mother, I really did try last week to make up. I said I was sorry. I really am. It just all had to come out. I shouldn't have mentioned Tony.

Maureen That really upset me. We've always done what we thought was best for you both. That's all a parent can do. Of course, I knew that theatricals meant a lot to you. But I never thought you'd want them to be your work, not when there was the mill.

Pause

Last week I went over to see Father Kerrigan and he helped me a lot. Made me see it as God's will. Well, I just wanted to say that first, before you go...

Jamie Go?

Maureen Up to the house. Official letter, stamped "Education Department, Wakefield". Came for you today. Second post, would you believe?

Jamie (*crossing with his coat to the car park door*) Oh my God. Why didn't you bring it down?

Maureen I thought you'd prefer to read it in private. Not here with everyone around. Don't be disappointed if they say...

Jamie If they say *no*? Oh yes, Mother, make no mistake about it, I will be disappointed. But that's what you want them to say, isn't it? If that were "God's will", then you wouldn't have any problems.

Jamie exits by the car park door

Eily and Celia enter from the stage door. Eily is smoking a cigarette

Maureen (*calling after Jamie—too late*) You don't understand—Jamie! (*She moves to the door and calls after him*) Jamie!

Eily Where's he gone?

Maureen (*closing the door*) Home. He won't be long.

Eily Margaret wanted a word.

Maureen isn't listening and crosses to the costume rail

Celia When will she have finished with Brendan?

Eily As soon as they've fixed the ground row. (*She sits R of the table*)

Celia (*crossing to the costume rail*) Where's mine, Auntie Maureen?

Maureen It's all right, love, it's downstairs. Thanks for reminding me. Can't concentrate tonight. I need to try it on now. (*She crosses to the cellar door and switches on the light*)

Brendan enters from the stage door

Celia (*following Maureen*) I'll give you a hand.
Brendan Celia!
Celia (*turning to Brendan; quietly*) I've got to talk to you.
Maureen (*off*) Celia!

Celia exits through the cellar door

Brendan (*after a pause; looking at his watch*) Look at the time. Charlie Mitchell will want to get over to the British Legion before closing time.
Eily I know. I've told Margaret. She's just got to finish some bits and pieces. She'll let him go soon.
Brendan Shall I give Charlie a hand? (*He crosses to the stage door*)
Eily (*stubbing out her cigarette*) No, he can manage. Cigarette? (*She rises*)
Brendan No, thanks.
Eily Very strong willed, aren't we?

Pause. Eily searches through the DS box

I thought I'd put them in here.
Brendan What?
Eily Me father's old boots. (*She looks at him*) They were for you. I told Maureen. (*She continues to search*)
Brendan Will they fit?
Eily (*finding the boots*) Yes, love—nine and a half.
Brendan How did you know?
Eily (*quickly*) I asked Celia—or was it Bridget? What decision did they make at the Pools Meeting?
Brendan (*hesitating*) They've booked a minibus for Blackpool on the last Saturday in June.
Eily Great. Mind you, after all those Saturdays, checking the results, we deserve it.
Brendan Eily?
Eily What is it?
Brendan I won't be going.
Eily Why not?
Brendan Because I resigned from the Committee last night.
Eily Why? I thought you enjoyed it?
Brendan Oh, I do. (*He pauses*) But, it's not fair on Celia.

Eily I've never heard her complain.
Brendan You know Celia. She's not the complaining type.
Eily (*after a pause*) Well, you'll be missed—every Saturday.
Brendan Will I?
Eily You know you will.
Brendan I think they'll soon find a replacement. I've suggested Charlie Mitchell.
Eily (*with difficulty*) Well, I will.
Brendan What?
Eily Miss you.
Brendan (*laughing it off*) You talk as if I were going to Siberia—I'll still be around. But...
Eily Yes?
Brendan I've got to spend more time with Celia. She needs me. She needs me to show her a bit more care—to give her a bit more attention.
Eily But you do?
Brendan No, not really. Until Paddy's Ball, if there's been any fun, any jokes, any chance to relax, I've chosen to share it with you. Don't get me wrong. I, we—just let it get a bit out of hand. So it's got to stop, otherwise I might have—we both might have regrets. You know?
Eily Has it been so noticeable?
Brendan It's been noticeable to me. Only me. And you've made me want to respond. Seeing you, being in your company, making arrangements, it's been like having a secret, inside, that you can't share with anyone—but it's a secret that makes you feel so good. That's before you've thought of ... the pain—that it can bring—to others.
Eily I'm sorry.
Brendan (*touching her shoulder*) There's nothing to be sorry for, that's the point.
Eily (*breaking away*) You're right. Absolutely right. Nothing to be sorry for! (*The boots are in her hand, tied together and she throws them at his feet. Her voice is slightly out of control*) Here are your boots.

Celia enters from the cellar

Don't clean them, dirty them up in the allotment.
Celia What's all this about? (*Joking*) What's he done wrong?
Eily (*now controlled*) He's not dirtied his boots.

Eily exits by the stage door

Celia Is she all right? She seems in a funny mood.
Brendan (*replacing the boots in one of the boxes*) You know Eily. Tension's

Act II, Scene 1

mounting, full dress rehearsal tomorrow—then it's muck or nettles on Saturday.
Celia Never mind Eily.

Pause

Well? I've been waiting for you. What were the results of your tests?
Brendan (*after a pause*) It's *me*. My sperm count's very low.
Celia You? Not me!
Brendan Don't say it like that.
Celia Oh, my God. *If only I'd known.* If only I'd known. What else did he say?
Brendan "With your sperm count, Mr O'Malley, it is highly unlikely that your wife will conceive." Those were his words.
Celia I see. So that's that. No magic injections?
Brendan No. He asked if we had considered adoption and I said *no*, we hadn't.
Celia Well—we didn't know.
Brendan That's what I said. (*He over-reacts*) Adoption's a serious decision. It wouldn't be our child.
Celia We'd make it ours.
Brendan (*angrily*) But we'd always know that it wasn't.
Celia (*charged by Brendan's attitude*) That's ridiculous. In no time at all you wouldn't ever think it was adopted. We would love her. Yes, I'd like a girl.
Brendan Celia, I don't think I'm ready to...
Celia It's all come as a bit of a shock. We'll talk about it. Promise? (*She links his arm*)
Brendan Yes. Promise.
Celia (*kissing his cheek*) Thanks. Why were you so late?
Brendan I just missed the early train. He was behind with his appointments. There were eight of us in the waiting room. Nobody spoke a word. It was as if the Infertility Clinic didn't exist—as if each man were saying to himself "I'm not here". After a while the main door opened and a man said: "Is this the foot specialist—bunions?" And I said "No. You've definitely come to the wrong place". We all laughed and then we started to talk—cleared the air.
Celia I bet it did.

Pause

I didn't tell your mother where you were.
Brendan Thanks. Has she heard about *her* tests?
Celia Yes.

Brendan What did the consultant say?
Celia All I know is that he's put her on a new prescription which seems to have taken her appetite away. Haven't you noticed?
Brendan No, I haven't.
Celia You're that unobservant.
Brendan Not so unobservant that I realize we need a break. A few days away together.
Celia Oh, yes! We can ask Eily to help out.
Brendan No. She's stage-managing Threshton Players' next show. Mother will see us right. I'll have a word with her.
Celia Well, only for a few days. I don't want your mother overdoing things. But why this decision?
Brendan I wanted to ... to do something special. You deserve it.
Celia And we will have time?

Brendan looks at her

You know? To make decisions?
Brendan Yes. I'm sorry if I've been a bit—irritable—unfriendly. Waiting for the results hasn't helped. It's been on my mind ... all the time and seeing the consultant hasn't made it any easier.
Celia It's been a difficult time (*she pauses*) for both of us. Everything's going to be all right.

Brendan takes out a cigarette

I know it is. (*Angrily*) And you don't need a cigarette—you said you'd given up?

Maureen enters from the cellar carrying Celia's costume. She turns out the cellar light and closes the door

Brendan (*over-reacting*) I said I was trying to cut down. I need this one. (*He lights it*)
Maureen That's right, you tick him off. I have to keep my eye on Jamie.
Celia There's always an excuse.

Bridget enters through the stage door

Bridget Excuse for what?
Celia (*controlling her emotion*) Oh, just something Brendan said. I think tonight we could all do with a cup of tea. I brought some milk earlier, just in case. Margaret won't mind?

Bridget Course she won't. We're all parched.

Paul enters from the stage door

Celia exits to the kitchen, puts on the light and closes the door

Paul Brendan—give us a hand with the netting. Margaret says it's casting too much shadow.
Brendan Right. I always said that netting would cause trouble.

Paul and Brendan exit by the stage door

Maureen meets Bridget's eye and crosses as if to exit to the cellar

Bridget Maureen, don't go. I've been up to see you at home three times. I think you were in. I'd hoped there'd be a chance to talk after rehearsals but you've slipped away early.

Pause

Maureen, I can understand how you feel but you've got to give me a chance to try to explain.

Pause

You said you'd known for two years.
Maureen I found a letter from you—to Joe. I found it just after he died.
Bridget So you've known all this time.
Maureen It happened when I took Tony to our Dorothy's in Grange—didn't it?

Bridget nods

Doctor Meadows liked the idea of Morecambe Bay, good air for his chest, something to do with the seaweed. (*Cynically*) Joe couldn't come, weaving parachutes—top priority, he said. Your Bill was overseas so it was all very convenient. We were only away a month. Yet long enough.

Pause

It was soon after we got back from Grange that I conceived Jamie. I was thirty-eight, remember, I didn't want another. I felt Joe forced it on me—having Jamie. (*Bitterly*) I think he wanted to start afresh, as if we were newly wed. You can't do that. When I found your letter it was as clear as daylight.

Bridget Maureen, it was just, something that happened, it took us by surprise. I made every effort to make certain that you'd never know. Joe and I made a promise: just before you returned from Grange. We agreed to avoid each other, as much as it was humanly possible, we would be strong, we wouldn't cheat. At Christmas, at family gatherings, at church do's, he was *always* there. It was hard. It was like that for about three years. Then one day, I don't know when it was, I didn't think about him, all day. And then gradually it got easier.

Pause

Maureen—I only cheated that once, with the letter. I wouldn't lie to you. Believe me. (*She tries to touch Maureen's arms*)

Maureen recoils

Margaret enters from the stage door with her director's copy

Maureen moves to the costume rail

Margaret Oh! That's been quite a marathon.
Bridget (*to Margaret*) Sit down, Margaret, and have a rest. Celia's making us a cuppa.
Margaret (*to Maureen*) Where's Jamie? (*She sits* US *at the head of the table*)
Maureen (*to Margaret*) He'll be back any minute. He had to go up home. The letter from Wakefield came today. I didn't like bringing it down here. I got into trouble about that. Nothing I do is right.
Bridget Well, only if they say "no" to the grant. If it were "yes" he'd love to be here with us all and we'd celebrate. (*To Margaret*) How much will it all cost? (*She sits* R *of the table*)
Margaret The fees and living in London—well, it will be close to three thousand pounds. Even with a grant he'll need to work in the vacations.
Bridget It's a lot of money.
Maureen (*changing the subject*) All the costumes are finished.
Margaret (*formally*) That's splendid. Thank you, Mrs Firth.
Maureen Not at all. (*She turns to Bridget*) We've only been too pleased to help.
Bridget Not so much of the we. You've done it all—at home.
Margaret (*first looking at Bridget and making an effort*) We are very glad that you decided to come back and help with the production.
Maureen Under the circumstances it was the least I could do.

Act II, Scene 1 53

Pause. Maureen sits L *of the table*

Miss Moorhouse, I owe you an apology. Saying the things I did. I—I even spoke to Reverend Mother. I shouldn't have done that. I'm sorry!
Margaret I know. She told me.
Maureen (*after a pause*) I'm that ashamed, I'm sorry.
Margaret Mrs Firth, when you made those accusations, about my relationship with Jamie, to my headmistress, you, how shall I put it? You started an enquiry which I should not have been subject to. You could have put my professional status in jeopardy. Serious jeopardy, Mrs Firth. In the educational world, a touch of scandal, however unjustified, can seriously affect one's position. And especially with a nun who is not really aware of the ways of the world and how attitudes have changed. Although she said she understood, I was put in a difficult, uncomfortable position having to justify my behaviour, having to account for my actions.
Maureen (*upset*) I really am sorry.
Celia (*off*) Tea's ready.

The hatch is opened and we see Celia—mugs of tea all ready on a tray

Margaret Thanks, Celia, it couldn't be more welcome. I'll get the others. (*She calls from the stage door*) Celia's made tea.
Sarah (*off*) We're coming.

In silence, Maureen and Bridget cross and get the tea. Maureen gives one mug to Margaret and keeps one for herself. Bridget takes out a letter from her handbag

Bridget Maureen, Tony's letter.
Maureen (*taking the letter*) Thanks.

Maureen and Bridget sit at opposite sides of the table

Paul, Sarah and Brendan come in from the stage door

Paul I'm dying for a cuppa.
Celia Come and get it.

They cross to the hatch for their tea

Sarah Me too. Thanks, Celia.
Margaret Where's Eily?
Paul She wasn't feeling too good. Sends her apologies. Asked me to give you

these notes. I think she's just exhausted and re-arranging the netting with Brendan seemed to be the last straw—a really long sleep and she'll be all right. (*He passes the notes to Margaret and crosses with his tea to look at the model of the set which is on the piano*)

Celia Yes. She's taken tomorrow off.

Paul I've got the half day so we've arranged to set up everything straight after lunch.

Margaret I could have taken her home in the car. (*She moves to the* US *head of the table*)

Sarah It's all right. Charlie Mitchell offered to drive her home.

Celia And she accepted? I won't half tease her about this tomorrow. That's what comes of dancing with him at Paddy's Ball.

Bridget You leave Eily alone. Why shouldn't Charlie Mitchell take her home—he's a grand chap. I'm surprised— (*she smiles*) but I'm right pleased!

Celia You old matchmaker.

Margaret (*rather tetchily*) Can we settle down? It's getting late.

They do

As Eily's gone home, there are one or two things I need to say: tomorrow's dress rehearsal will be in the actual running order for the concert. So please, I want the actors here by seven fifteen. Because of the festival next Monday, I've arranged a Sunday run here on the stage, same time. A friend of Paul's is coming down from the Lake District to see it—and he knows the play.

Paul Well, he hopes to come down. I should warn you that he saw the Abbey Theatre Company do it.

Bridget (*laughing*) Well, I'd rather not think about that!

Margaret We have tickets for the final Saturday. There are only two plays before the adjudication, so it won't be a long evening.

Celia After the results are announced, couldn't we have a little "do" here, a kind of party, even to commiserate!

Bridget I think that's a grand idea. I'll lay on something special.

Brendan What about your steak and kidney pie?

Bridget You're on.

Celia (*to Sarah*) Bridget's a dab hand with puff pastry.

Brendan And wine—on the house.

Maureen I could bake a chocolate cake.

Sarah I could make a flower arrangement—and some candles. Shall I?

Bridget That's right, Sarah. You do that. A real celebration. (*She rises to put her mug on the kitchen shelf*)

Margaret It'll be just us plus Jamie—and Eily of course. The others are going to the Catenian Ball in Harrogate.

Act II, Scene 1   55

Sarah Iris told me about the Ball. The tickets are very expensive, so they don't want to get there late.
Bridget It's years since Bill took me. We always used to go in a foursome with Maureen and Joe... (*She catches Maureen's eye*) And then we stopped going, you know how it is. (*She stands behind her chair*) It's a grand affair. Evening dress and all that. I love to see a man in a dinner jacket and bow tie, it gives them style. Wonderful marble staircase as you go in. Silver service meal, white damask tablecloths and flowers everywhere. Palm trees in the conservatory, coloured lights, big orchestra *and* a céilé band. (*She sings*)
> Oh the days of the Kerry dancing!
> Oh the ring of the piper's tune!
> Oh for one of those hours of gladness,
> Gone, alas! like our youth too soon. (*She is close to tears*)

They applaud and Bridget sits

Unnoticed, the car park door has opened and Jamie enters

The applause peters out when they see Jamie

Margaret (*rising*) Well?
Jamie No grant.
Margaret That's terrible.
Bridget I can't believe it.
Sarah I'm sorry, Jamie.
Brendan Feel like writing to our County Councillor.
Celia Good idea.
Paul It's Mrs Fletcher and she's not very keen on the arts—you'd be wasting your time.
Sarah What else can you do?
Jamie Have a flag day.
Sarah Seriously.
Jamie I don't know. I'll have to think.
Margaret Did you ask about scholarships at RADA?
Jamie Yes. I phoned last week. They've all been awarded. I was lucky to be seen. Remember I was very late applying.
Maureen (*rising*) I can think of only one thing.

They all turn to Maureen

Jamie What, Mother?
Maureen (*crossing to his side*) Put it to your Uncle Ernest. Explain it all. At

a pinch he might let us sell some of our shares. But *you* do it. It's better coming from you, as Joe's son. Tell him I want his support, his help.
Jamie (*touched by her gesture*) Thanks, Mother. But I've got an idea that Uncle Ernest has other priorities. Nevertheless I'll put it to him tomorrow.
Paul All fingers crossed.
Margaret Yes, Jamie, you can't give up now.
Sarah (*putting on her coat*) It's late. I'm sorry, but I'll have to go. Mother's not so well.
Bridget I'm sorry, love.
Jamie I'll see you home.
Paul (*picking up his portfolio*) I'll come with you as far as the Springs' Canal Bridge.
Celia Two's company, three's a crowd!
Paul (*laughing*) Only as far as the bridge. (*He looks at Jamie*) I know when I'm not wanted.
Jamie (*to Paul*) Come along. (*To the rest*) Goodnight.
Paul
Sarah } (*together*) Goodnight.

Paul and Sarah exit by the stage door

Margaret (*rising and crossing to Jamie*) Jamie, if there is anything I could do, you know that I would do it.
Jamie I know, Margaret. Thanks. (*He turns to Maureen*) I won't be long, Mother. Wait up for me.
Maureen I will.

Jamie exits by the stage door

Silence

Margaret I really thought he'd get a grant.
Bridget I can't bear it.
Celia Poor Jamie. (*She puts mugs on the tray*)

Brendan helps her, and Maureen sorts out the shoes and boots in one of the boxes

(*Making conversation*) I'll wash these up tomorrow. I said I'd pop over at lunchtime to give Eily and Paul a hand.

Celia exits to the kitchen

All apart from Maureen start to put on their coats and collect bags etc.

Act II, Scene 1   57

Margaret It was a tough technical but we got through everything—Charlie Mitchell and Eily were wonderful. Well, you all were. It's been a long day. And now Jamie's bad news.

Celia closes the kitchen hatch

Brendan Come on then, Mother. Are you all right? (*He helps Bridget into her coat*)

Bridget Of course I'm all right. It's just that my mind's racing away. I don't know if I'll sleep with Jamie on my mind.

Celia enters from the kitchen with her coat, turns out the kitchen light and closes the door

Celia Brendan can give you a special night cap.
Bridget Do you know I just might weaken. I want a word with Maureen.
Brendan Goodnight, Auntie Maureen.

Maureen nods and turns out the gas fire

Celia Goodnight, love. Don't be long.
Maureen No. I've just got one or two things to sort out. Goodnight, Miss Moorhouse.
Margaret Goodnight.

Celia and Margaret exit through the car park door

Brendan Don't forget the lights or you'll have George Wilton on to you.

Brendan exits through the car park door

Bridget I just wanted to say...
Maureen No. Not now. I've had about as much as I can take tonight...
Bridget Would you like me to walk you home?
Maureen No. Over the years I've had to learn to look after myself. I'll just get me sewing things together.
Bridget (*at the car park door*) Right, I'll see you for the Dress Rehearsal. 'Night, Maureen.

Maureen nods

Bridget exits by the car park door

Pause

Maureen crosses US *for her coat, which she puts on, and her kerchief. She picks up her sewing bag and switches off the* US *lights and crosses* DS *to collect her handbag*

Bridget enters from the car park door

Maureen.
Maureen You gave me a shock.

Pause

What is it?

Pause

Bridget It's Tony. He's in the car park. He's come home.
Maureen Come home?
Bridget He's given up his vocation. He's in a bit of a state—you know, upset. Waiting for everyone to go. I think it's better if I don't come out with you. I'll go the front way.

Pause

Maureen, be gentle with him, try to understand, try to forget your disappointment.
Maureen Disappoint... This is the saddest day of my life.
Bridget Try to think of it as the happiest. He's back. Back home.

Pause

Oh, Maureen, try. (*She touches Maureen's arm*)

Maureen meets Bridget's eye and she recoils, and the Lights swiftly fade to Black-out

Scene 2

In a short while the Lights come up and it is nine days later, 10.30 pm Saturday evening

The company of eight (Maureen is absent) are casually seated around a trestle table angled RC *where the remains of their supper can be seen*

Act II, Scene 2

Bridget is UR, *facing Jamie* DL. *Paul, Margaret and Brendan sit* US *of the table, and Eily, Celia and Sarah sit* DS *of the table. The company have gone to some trouble regarding what to wear for the final adjudication which they have recently attended, and Eily is in a ball gown*

The steak and kidney pie and plates etc. have been cleared to the kitchen. Half of Maureen's large cake is left, it is surrounded by 4 candles in small candlesticks, in the centre of the table. Everyone has a wine glass and Sarah's two white rose floral arrangements are towards both ends of the table which is covered by a white damask cloth. To the left of the large table, near the piano, are two card tables with coloured cloths and some lit candles, two silver trophies are on display. By the side of these tables is a chair and two bottles of wine, one unopened, another opened bottle of wine is DS *on the kitchen shelf*

There is a row of lit colourful paper lanterns hanging from the ceiling, hence the room looks warm and colourful. The kitchen hatch is closed and there are some lit candles on the kitchen hatch shelf

As the Lights come up on the scene they are laughing at the story that Bridget is telling. Celia is standing US *of table, holding the used dessert plates and forks*

Bridget ...and then he said, (*claiming their attention*) then he said: (*with a mock RP accent*) "Maurya needed to look older".

Laughter

Needed to look older. I'm about ten years too old for the part.
Sarah I don't care what you say—he signed my programme. (*She holds the programme*)

Teasing from the boys

Eily Bridget, you should know that any self-respecting actress can knock off ten years on the stage. Why do you think all those film stars, in their late forties, start a new career on the stage?
Celia It's an attempt to look like the proverbial thirty-nine. (*She puts the plates on the kitchen hatch shelf*)
Paul Then later on they can have a face lift (*he uses both hands to "lift" up his face*) and go on for another ten years. Men don't do that.
Celia Men don't need to. Look at Cary Grant. As far as I'm concerned he's been twenty-nine for years.

Bridget I like Cary Grant. Style.
Celia (*sitting at the table*) You can say that again.
Bridget The flowers are beautiful, Sarah. I love white roses. (*To Jamie*) You did ask your mother to join us?
Jamie Yes. She said she'd see how things were with Tony.
Bridget I was right glad she came down to the Town Hall to hear the results.
Jamie She just doesn't like leaving him on his own for too long, he's still depressed. Bit of a nervous breakdown.
Celia Auntie Maureen says he doesn't want to see anyone.
Jamie No, he doesn't. It could be that he went to the seminary for the wrong reasons—an escape route. Anyway, Mother's having a difficult time and I suppose I'm not helping 'cos of my problems.
Bridget (*to Jamie*) She was that upset when your Uncle Ernest wouldn't help.
Jamie He's been thinking about it for a week but ... he needs the money for automatic looms.
Sarah Never mind. Don't let it spoil tonight's celebrations.
Bridget Your mother was right thrilled that *Riders* won.
Margaret (*rising*) And I was thrilled that you got the best actress award.

General enthusiastic approval

It was richly deserved! You have a natural talent, Bridget, (*she looks at Jamie*) which seems to be in the family. Ladies and Gentlemen—a toast to Bridget, actress of distinction.

They all except Bridget rise and toast her, using Margaret's words. This is followed by applause and "speech—speech" coming from Jamie and Paul and so they resume their seats

Bridget (*rising*) I don't know what to say. I can't find the words. (*She moves behind her chair*)
Paul That'll be the day.

Laughter

Bridget (*genially*) Less of that, young Paul. What I mean is...

Pause

I've never before had the chance to act in something so serious, so powerful. I've always either been the clown in the comic sketches or singing in musical comedies and now, at long last, I've had the chance to be in a classical play—you know like being at the Old Vic! You helped me

Act II, Scene 2

to really identify with Maurya; more than you'll ever know. Thank you for all the lovely things you have said. But it couldn't have happened without you. I don't just mean my performance—I mean the whole production.

"Hear-hear" from the others

Sarah? (*She indicates the kitchen*)

Sarah exits quickly, returning with a bouquet of flowers

We didn't know what to get you. This is just a small gesture, Sarah's idea, of our appreciation and love.
Sarah To Margaret—the best producer. (*She gives Margaret the bouquet*)

They all reiterate "Margaret—the best producer"

Margaret (*rising*) Thank you, Bridget. Sarah. Thank you all. It seems a long time ago since Father Kerrigan asked me over to the presbytery to discuss a festival play...

The car park door opens and Maureen stands there, hesitant

They all turn to face her. Pause

Mrs Firth. We're so glad that you could come down. (*She places the bouquet on the card table*)

Maureen hangs up her coat by the notice board

Bridget Yes, Maureen. Jamie explained. We're right glad to see you.
Brendan (*gesturing*) Seat for you, Auntie Maureen.

Maureen sits in Brendan's chair next to Jamie, and Margaret returns to her seat between Maureen and Paul

Wine?
Maureen Just a drop, thanks. I'm only staying for a minute.
Sarah As you can see, Mrs Firth, your chocolate cake has been enjoyed...
Celia Would you like some?

Brendan gives Maureen a glass of wine

Maureen No, thanks. (*She raises her glass*) I just wanted to congratulate you on winning the festival.

Margaret Thank you, Mrs Firth.
Brendan Don't forget Mother? (*He sits on the chair near the card tables and pours himself another glass of wine*)
Maureen That didn't surprise me. Even way back in Listowel Dad always said she was a born actress.
Bridget (*laughing*) I don't know what you mean by that Maureen. Anyway, I've decided to go to Listowel next week. Just for five days.
Maureen But why?
Bridget Got a sudden urge to go down memory lane.
Brendan You do right. It will do you good.
Bridget But I got sidetracked. Margaret was saying something—to us all—Margaret?
Margaret (*rising*) Working with you all on *Riders* has given me tremendous pleasure. It will always remind me of my time in Threshton. Unfortunately, this will be my last play here. I am leaving in July, I've got a post in one of the new comprehensive schools in Bristol. It should be quite a challenge.
Jamie Why aren't you staying on at St Monica's?
Margaret Reverend Mother didn't ask me.
Eily (*rising and pouring herself a glass of wine from the bottle on the kitchen shelf*) She must be mad. Doesn't she know a good thing when she sees it? Wish you'd been my teacher, (*she leans on the kitchen wall*) then I might have gone to university and not be stuck in the showroom in Threshton.
Margaret It's never too late to change direction, Eily. (*She sits*)
Eily Oh, yes. It's far too late.
Bridget Cheer up, love, you're going to enjoy the ball. (*She rises and stands behind her chair*) I've got something important to say. Maureen, when I heard at the Town Hall that Ernest Firth wouldn't help Jamie—well, I couldn't get it out of my mind and I think I've found the answer. It's been difficult to wait until now, (*to Maureen*) but I wanted you, all of you, to be here together. Jamie, when I sold the shop half went to help Brendan and Celia and the other half went to David to set up his business in Melbourne. I kept something back for me old age. It's just enough to see you through your time at RADA.
Jamie But Auntie Bridget, I can't...
Bridget No. Let me finish. I don't want you to feel that you are depriving me of any comforts of me old age. I'm letting you have it as a loan. It may take you a long time to pay it off but I can wait, there's no hurry. And if I were to fall under a bus tomorrow then the money's yours, so you don't have to feel insecure during your time in London. So you see tonight's a real celebration. (*To Maureen*) *Riders* has been a special journey for all of us but particularly for Jamie. Tonight is really his night and the final toast is to him. (*She rises*) To Jamie with my love and every success for the future.

Act II, Scene 2   63

*They all, except Maureen, reiterate "To Jamie—success for the future".
Bridget sits*

Jamie I don't know what to say. I'd given up all hope. And now comes this (*he searches for the word*) reprieve. How can I ever thank you?
Bridget Just making a success of the course will be thanks enough.
Jamie Whether I make a success of it is in the lap of the gods. But you have made it possible. (*He crosses to her side*) You've always been a guardian angel to me. Some of my happiest times have been with you. You've always encouraged me. Thank you for everything, Auntie Bridget. For all you've done for me. (*He kisses her*)
Bridget (*moved*) Now then. Enough's been said.

A car horn is heard from the car park

Eily That'll be Charlie. (*She crosses to the* DL *hooks for her coat*)
Celia Enjoy it. You look lovely.
Eily Thanks. I will. (*To Brendan*) Don't forget that George Wilton wants to lock up soon after eleven but you don't have to clear up until morning.
Celia All right, love; you'll be the belle of the ball. Is Charlie going to drive?
Eily Yes. I've already had too much wine. (*She crosses over to Celia and kisses her cheek*)
Celia What was that for?
Eily I just felt like it.
Celia Have a lovely time.
Jamie I hope he hasn't been all this time in the British Legion.
Brendan (*with bitterness*) You know how he likes his drink.
Eily (*protesting too much*) No, he hasn't. He just went home to change—into his dinner jacket. (*She starts to put on her coat*)
Celia It's all right, love. No-one's getting at you—or Charlie.
Eily (*picking up her evening handbag from the piano*) Enjoy the rest of the celebration.
Bridget We will.
Margaret And thanks for the lanterns, Eily.
Brendan Sorry I couldn't help you.
Eily I managed. I'm glad you like them.
Bridget They're lovely. (*She looks at them*) A little touch of magic…
Eily Magic? Oh, yes.

The horn sounds again

   Ta-ra.
Bridget Enjoy yourself. You're only young once.

Eily exits by the car park door

Celia She's a bit edgy, what's got into her?
Bridget Nerves. It's her first proper date with Charlie. She's all churned up. Poor lass.
Paul Some wine, Margaret?
Margaret No, thanks. Everyone else has provided for tonight's celebration, except me. I've given Brendan and Celia some champagne, so please come over to the Guest House for a final drink. I hope you'll come.
Paul You're on! Terrific.
Sarah Thank you, Margaret.
Margaret (*rising*) Before we go over, I'd like to give Jamie a small gift. (*She takes a parcel from the piano*) It's only a book. (*She gives it to him*) I bought it really to cheer you up. But now the title is an omen for the future.
Paul Open it.
Jamie Give me a chance. (*He opens the parcel and passes the wrapping paper to Sarah*)
Paul Well?
Jamie *A Life in the Theatre*—Tyrone Guthrie.
Bridget That's lovely.
Margaret I've written something in it.

Jamie opens the flap and reads the inscription

Jamie Oh Margaret. I'll try to live up to your words. Thank you for everything. I'm going to miss you very much. (*He embraces her*)

Margaret is visibly moved

Celia I'm going to cry. Come on, let's go over.
Paul The champagne calls!
Brendan Yes. Leave everything. Celia and I will clear up in the morning.

Celia blows out the candles on the kitchen shelf. They gather up their coats etc.

Sarah What an evening. (*To Jamie*) I'm thrilled for you and you deserve it, Jamie. Really.
Jamie Thanks, Sarah.
Paul Margaret—don't forget your trophy.
Margaret *Our* trophy. (*She picks it up*)
Paul We'll have to fill it with champagne. Photos in *Picture-Goer*.

Margaret picks up her bouquet

Act II, Scene 2 65

Brendan Are you coming, Auntie Maureen? (*To Paul*) We haven't got a camera!
Paul I'll run home and get mine. (*He rushes to Bridget*) I think you're wonderful.
Bridget God love you.

Paul goes out

Maureen No, Brendan. It's late. Before I go, I'd like to have a minute with you Bridget.
Jamie (*to Maureen*) I'm sorry you're not coming over, but I understand.
Maureen (*meaningfully*) Do you?
Jamie Of course I do—Tony.
Sarah (*crossing to Jamie and taking his hand*) Come on, Jamie. Margaret, come on!

Jamie, Sarah and Margaret go out through the stage door

Celia Don't forget the lights. (*She sees Brendan with a glass in his hand*) Come on, love. We've left the van in the car park.

Celia and Brendan exit through the car park door

Bridget and Maureen are left alone. Silence

Bridget What is it?
Maureen You've no idea, have you?
Bridget I know it must be difficult for you at the moment with Tony. Give him time and he'll recover. You didn't lose him after all.
Maureen It wasn't a question of losing him, Bridget. To give him to the service of the church wasn't losing him. But I haven't been able to face the parish. I bet the tongues are wagging. You know what they say: (*quietly*) "Pity he's a spoiled priest".
Bridget Stop it, Maureen. It's none of their business. Don't let them see that you care. Concentrate on caring about Tony. "Spoiled"—he simply found out that the priesthood wasn't for him. (*She smiles*) Help him and Jamie to make a fresh start.
Maureen That's what I've been trying to do, that's why for Jamie I made the effort to come down here tonight. And what happens? Auntie Bridget becomes his guardian angel. I find myself humiliated again, in front of everyone.
Bridget Maybe my timing wasn't very good. I'm sorry. You know what you often say: "God moves in a mysterious way"—well, maybe He has. Tony

comes back to you and Jamie's all set to leave. It's a fair exchange. I wouldn't complain.

Maureen This "loan" puts him in "Auntie Bridget's debt" which is where you want him to be. You heard him, you're the one with whom he's spent "some of his happiest times".

Bridget It was just his way of showing appreciation.

Maureen It was more than that. He more or less ignored me.

Bridget He just got carried away. Can't you remember what it was like? We loved our parents but did we always consider them? If you wanted to do something, Maureen, you did it. In Jamie's excitement, you were briefly overlooked; he had his whole future, there in his grasp—it was his moment, you couldn't expect it to be yours.

Maureen Nevertheless, it didn't stop you being part of "his moment". (*She meets Bridget's eye*) Like father like son.

Pause

Bridget Maybe I reached out to Jamie as a way of holding on to Joe. I don't know. Without you knowing I've always tried to make it up to you. I didn't intend to cause you pain, Maureen.

Maureen The real pain for me is that Joe kept your letter for all those years.

Bridget I can't help that. It's something you'll have to accept. But he was a good man. He loved you. I simply watched from the sidelines. For eighteen years. A lifetime. I want to make it up to you. I want you to forgive me.

Maureen It's not as easy as that, Bridget, making up? To forgive and forget? I can't wave some magic wand and pretend it never happened? You can't expect me to wipe the slate clean—just like that. It'll take time. A lot of time.

Bridget Sit down, Maureen. (*She places a chair* DL) There's something important that I want to tell you. I want to tell you because in spite of everything I want us to be friends—like we used to be.

Maureen sits and Bridget places another chair next to Maureen's and sits.
Pause

(*Matter-of-factly*) I've got cancer. The consultant gives me eight or nine months at the most. So you see, time is the one thing I haven't got much of. No-one else must know, not yet. Not until they have to. I want you to promise that.

Maureen nods her head

Act II, Scene 2

I don't want to be a burden to those that I love. I want to enjoy each day for as long as I can. And I want to make my peace.

Maureen tries to speak

Don't say anything. As sisters we've always known what not to say. Remember when we first came over and they called us "The Kerry Sisters"?

Maureen nods

So now you know why I'm going to Listowel.

The Lights slowly close in on the two sisters who are sitting closely together

Maureen Where will you stay?
Bridget The Listowel Arms. It's three stars now.
Maureen You know what they always say: "Never go back", you might find it very upsetting.
Bridget No, I won't. I'm going to say goodbye, that's all. There's so much I want to see. The river. Remember where we used to swim with Dorothy?
Maureen Dear Dorothy. (*She makes the sign of the cross*) May she—rest... (*She stops, embarrassed*)
Bridget ...in peace. Amen.

From now onwards they do not look at each other and readily slip into the Kerry accent

That year the soldiers camped down by the bridge. You flirted with them like crazy. You were outrageous.
Maureen I wasn't!
Bridget Mo Walsh, you were outrageous. Thank goodness you had me as a chaperone. Same at the Céilís at Flanagans.
Maureen Young Father Burke—on the violin.
Bridget You had a crush on him.
Maureen You always exaggerate. Mind you, if mother had heard that we'd gone swimming near to the camp...
Bridget But she didn't. Running across the fields to meet them. Dorothy got off with that Corporal.
Maureen Handsome man, blonde, curly hair. Went to the Picture Palace together in Tralee.
Bridget Seats on the back row. "An occasion of sin, Father".

They laugh

Maureen Oh Bridie, you're terrible.
Bridget I want to see Sullivan's Emporium.
Maureen It'll have changed.
Bridget Never mind, I know exactly where it is.
Maureen Centre of William Street. I used to bring you your lunches.
Bridget "Bridget Walsh on the Haberdashery Counter". Mrs Sullivan said I was wonderful with the customers. She didn't want me to leave to come to England.
Maureen Or to leave the choir. She was a great conductor.
Bridget Mam on the front row leading the sopranos.
Maureen Dad at the back in his Garda uniform.
Bridget When you were little holding your hand.
Maureen Took us on the pilgrimage.
Bridget Craugh Patrick—what a mountain.

They both look up—as if taking in the mountain

Maureen Barefooted.
Bridget On that long, steep path.
Maureen Penance.
Bridget Absolution?

Pause

Maureen Yes! On the top of the world.

Pause

Bridget Amen!
Maureen (*looking at Bridget*) We got lost.
Bridget (*looking at Maureen*) We went back. It's been a long time.

The Lighting returns to its previous level and they return to their Yorkshire accents. Pause

> I've decided to take up David's offer and go to Australia, I can't wait till Christmas, so I'm going in August. I've insisted that Brendan and Celia have a holiday.

Maureen I'll give you a hand with the beds.
Bridget It's all right. Celia's got Mary Devlin to come over. But thank you (*meaningfully*) for everything. You've taken a great weight off my mind.

Act II, Scene 2

Pause

Would you do me a special favour?
Maureen If I can, I will.
Bridget Go up home and try to persuade Tony to come down for that glass of champagne. Let's all be together, like old times.

They are standing close together, Bridget holds out her arms and in a moment Maureen goes to her and holds her very close. Pause

The stage door opens and Margaret enters

Margaret (*to Bridget*) I'm sorry to interrupt but we're waiting for you to come over so that we can open the champagne.

Maureen puts on her coat

(*To Maureen*) Actually, Jamie sent me over to see if I could persuade you to join us. He doesn't want you to be left out!
Bridget You see. I told you.

Pause

Please, Maureen?

Maureen buttons up her coat and puts on her kerchief and they wait

Maureen Well, tell them to wait another ten minutes and I'll do my best to bring Tony down with me. (*She goes to the car park door and turns*) I don't want it unless it's chilled.

Maureen exits

Margaret and Bridget gently laugh

Margaret How did you do it?
Bridget Shall we say—there was a mutual "shriving" and I think we gave each other absolution. (*She sighs and fastens her coat*)
Margaret Are you very tired?
Bridget No. Content. And you?
Margaret Tired? No. Content? Not really. It's right that I should move on. (*She meets Bridget's eye*)
Bridget I understand—*Jamie*?

Pause

Margaret I've been so careful.
Bridget Yes—it was only tonight.
Margaret The others?
Bridget No. Far too much wrapped in their own thoughts—never fear.
Margaret Ridiculous—isn't it?
Bridget No, it's not ridiculous. He's a lovely lad. I can understand.
Margaret He's so like someone I loved. He died in the last year of the War. But I'm no longer young, I'm a middle-aged, foolish woman caught in some kind of time warp. I should have known better... Yes, I have to move on.
Bridget Time plays tricks on us all. Come back and see me—have a little holiday?
Margaret That would be lovely. Next spring?
Bridget (*after a pause*) It's a busy time. Why not make it your October half term?
Margaret I'd love to.
Bridget Let's make that a definite booking. Now for the champagne.
Margaret The "chilled" champagne.

They laugh and Bridget takes a pace towards the stage door

Don't forget your trophy.

Bridget crosses to it, picks it up and holds it away from her as if receiving it from some dignitary

Bridget It's just like the Oscars. It's going to have pride of place on the mantelpiece. (*She holds it in her arms*)
Margaret You can't keep it, you know. You only have it for a year.
Bridget A year will be long enough.
Margaret Come on. They are all waiting. (*She blows out the candles on the card table*)

They cross to the stage door

We've forgotten the candles...

Bridget turns to look

...round the cake.
Bridget It looks like a birthday. (*She gives Margaret her trophy and crosses*

Act II, Scene 2

to the table) So it's my turn to wish. (*She closes her eyes, pauses, and then blows the candles out. Visibly moved, she joins Margaret at the stage door*)

Margaret turns off the lantern lights and they exit

Immediately, the Light fades in on Jamie, isolated by the piano and we faintly hear the piano accompaniment for The Kerry Dance

Jamie Bridget died just before Christmas. Dear Bridget. I so miss you.

Pause

On rostra level we see Bridget holding out her arms and facing Maureen

She got to Australia and was cheerful to the end. Mother took it very badly, they became really close in the last months.

The Light fades on Bridget and Maureen

Tony got better, returned to the mill and married Lizzie Bottomly—Paul's old girlfriend. Unfortunately for Mother, the mill went bust last year. Tony didn't mind. They emigrated to Melbourne to work with Bridget's David. Most of the "satanic" mills in Threshton have gone now and it's become a Dales tourist town. The guest house is flourishing.

On rostra level we see Celia linking Brendan's arm—as in Act II, Scene 1

Brendan and Celia couldn't adopt a baby, the authorities said they were too old. But there was worse to come. (*He pauses*) About five years ago Brendan suddenly left home, didn't tell anyone, just disappeared without trace. Why does someone you think you know so well do a thing like that?

The Lights fade on Celia and Brendan

It's taken its toll on Celia—yet she still hopes that one day he'll be there, standing at the door—that's love for you.

On rostra level we see Margaret holding the text of The Cherry Orchard—*as if directing a sequence from Jamie's audition speech*

Margaret got a university post in Edinburgh and directs plays for the drama society. I haven't seen her for years.

The Lights fade on Margaret

She always sends a Christmas card. Eily married Charlie Mitchell. They settled near Manchester.

On rostra level we see Eily shaking Brendan's hand—the "Catholic hand of honour" from Act II, Scene 1

Evidently Charlie became an alcoholic and refused to get help. Eily used to write to us, but we haven't heard from her for a number of years and someone in the parish told Mother that she had left him and gone South.

The Lights fade on Eily and Brendan. Pause

Paul qualified at Art School and went to live with Bob Hurndall and then they split up.

On rostra level we see Paul admiring the set design model for Riders to the Sea

He's in London now, in advertising. There's a new man in his life—a doctor. (*He pauses*) Wish you were here, Paul.

The Lights fade on Paul

After RADA and a lot of "resting", I was lucky to get work with various Reps. Now I'm here adjudicating the festival. They think I'm a bit of a celebrity. I've been on TV, small part in *The Forsyte Saga*—local boy makes good. Hardly a success story!

On rostra level we see Sarah alone holding the bouquet as if presenting it to Margaret

I didn't marry Sarah. At the time I convinced myself that I didn't want the commitment (*with meaning*) the story of my life!

The Lights fade on Sarah

She got engaged to that relief manager at the Building Society. (*He smiles*) They had a big wedding reception at The Midland. (*He picks up the flowers*) These roses were for Auntie Bridget but she always said flowers should be for the living. I'll take them up to Mother. Poor Mother. Bridget would like that.

He turns and takes a pace US *and sees a tableau, dimly lit, of all the characters*

round the supper table. It is the moment when only Bridget is standing and about to say "To Jamie with my love and every success for the future". Jamie crosses to the festival celebration table and stands next to Bridget

(*Slowly and with concern*) Everything is going to be all right, Auntie Bridget—*isn't it*? (*He goes towards the stage doors, and takes a final look at the room*)

The tableau starts to fade slowly. We have a final brief glimpse of the tableau and Jamie as the piano music fades and so to Black-out

CURTAIN

FURNITURE AND PROPERTY LIST

Further dressing may be added at the director's discretion

ACT I

Scene 1

On stage: Deep shelf in kitchen hatch
Shelves and domestic properties in kitchen
Rostrum
Gobos
Practical central gas fire
9 undistinguished wooden chairs
1 wooden desk chair with arms
Old desk/table
Stacked card tables
1 upright card table
Old upright piano. *On it*: statue of the Virgin Mary
Piano stool
2 rows of clothes hooks
Notice board. *On it*: poster for St Patrick's Ball
3 large central lights, with faded green metal shades
Light above the notice board

Off stage: White roses (**Jamie**)
Shopping bag with matches, script, clip file, masking tape, measurer (**Eily**)
Tin of biscuits (**Celia**)
Cardboard box containing ground plan, brochure, white paper (**Paul**)
Record player, LP record (**Jamie**)
Handbag with letter, shopping bag containing milk, tea, sugar (**Maureen**)
Tray with tea things and biscuits (**Maureen**)
Trolley with large tea pot, milk jug and sugar basin (**Maureen**)
Briefcase containing script and duplicated rehearsal schedule sheets(**Margaret**)
Handbags and coats and matching scripts

Furniture and Property List

Personal: **Jamie:** wet mackintosh, watch (worn throughout)
Eily: watch (worn throughout)
Bridget: handkerchief
Paul: Art Course brochure

Scene 2

Set: 2 beer crates containing empty bottles
Used glasses
Bottles
Metal dustbin
Eily's shopping bag containing thermos, 2 cups
Eily's umbrella
Faded small shamrock harp
Ashtray on DL card table and also on old desk/table

Off stage: Handbag, script (**Margaret**)
Wet umbrella (**Bridget**)
Shopping bag with sewing materials (**Maureen**)

Personal: **Brendan:** packet of ten cigarettes, matches
Paul: packet of cigarettes
Margaret: wet mackintosh

ACT II

Scene 1

Set: Costume rail with costumes
2 boxes of boots and shoes
Large bin
Small ground row laid out on newspaper
Pot of dark green paint
Drawing of ground row
Speaker
Coat and kerchief
Sewing bag
Handbag
Ashtray on old desk/table
Poster for the Parish Concert on notice board
Poster for the Drama Festival on US kitchen wall by the hatch
Paul's set design model on top of piano

Off stage:	Paintbrush (**Paul**)
	Pin cushion, **Sarah**'s skirt (**Maureen**)
	Celia's skirt (**Maureen**)
	Script (**Margaret**)
	Tray with mugs of tea (**Celia**)
	Handbag containing letter (**Bridget**)
Personal:	**Eily:** cigarette
	Brendan: watch, cigarette
	Bridget: letter
	Paul: Eily's notes

Scene 2

Set:	Half of **Maureen**'s large cake, surrounded by 4 candles in small candlesticks
	Glasses of wine
	White damask cloth on table
	2 white rose floral arrangements on table
	2 card tables with coloured cloths and some lit candles
	2 silver trophies
	Chair
	2 empty bottles of wine
	Unopened bottle of wine
	Opened bottle of wine
	Colourful paper lanterns hanging from ceiling
	Lit candles
	Used dessert plates and forks
	Programme
	Eily's evening handbag on piano
	Parcel on piano
	Coats for characters on US and DS clothes hooks
Off stage:	Bouquet of flowers (**Sarah**)
	Script (**Margaret**)
	Set design model (**Paul**)

LIGHTING PLOT

Practical fittings required: kitchen light, cellar light, lanterns
1 interior. The same throughout

ACT I, SCENE 1

To open:	Spotlight on **Jamie**	
Cue 1	During **Jamie**'s speech *Slowly bring up lights*	(Page 1)
Cue 2	**Jamie** crosses to the window *Start to fade general lighting*	(Page 2)
Cue 3	We hear Britten's *Moonlight* *Atmospherical lighting on three characters from Riders to the Sea—everything else in darkness*	(Page 2)
Cue 4	**Cathleen** kneels. Tableau *Fade lights*	(Page 2)
Cue 5	**Eily** switches on DS lights *Turn on DS lights*	(Page 2)
Cue 6	**Eily** switches on US lights *Turn on US lights*	(Page 2)
Cue 7	**Eily** switches on cellar light *Turn on cellar light*	(Page 5)
Cue 8	**Eily** switches off cellar light *Turn off cellar light*	(Page 6)
Cue 9	**Maureen** switches on kitchen light *Turn on kitchen light*	(Page 11)
Cue 10	**Margaret**: "…of the piece in its entirety." *Very gradually focus on them all*	(Page 22)

Cue 11 The music swells (Page 23)
          Fade to black-out

ACT I, SCENE 2

To open: Overall lighting of a rainy afternoon, cellar light on

Cue 12 Paul switches off cellar light (Page 26)
          Turn off celler light

Cue 13 Paul switches on the DS lights (Page 29)
          Turn on DS lights

Cue 14 Bridget starts to cry (Page 38)
          Fade lights to black-out

ACT II, SCENE 1

To open: Spotlight on **Jamie** and cellar light on

Cue 15 **Jamie**: "…before the end of the year." (Page 39)
          Fade light on **Jamie***; in a moment bring up atmospheric stage lighting from* UR

Cue 16 **Jamie** switches on the DS lights (Page 40)
          Turn on DS lights

Cue 17 **Eily** switches on the US light (Page 45)
          Turn on US light

Cue 18 **Maureen** switches off cellar light (Page 45)
          Turn off cellar light

Cue 19 **Maureen** switches on cellar light (Page 47)
          Turn on cellar light

Cue 20 **Maureen** switches off cellar light (Page 50)
          Turn off cellar light

Cue 21 **Celia** switches on kitchen light (Page 51)
          Turn on kitchen light

Lighting Plot

Cue 22	**Celia** switches off kitchen light *Turn off kitchen light*	(Page 57)
Cue 23	**Maureen** switches off the US light *Turn off US light*	(Page 58)
Cue 24	**Maureen** meets **Bridget**'s eye *Fade swiftly to black-out*	(Page 58)

ACT II, SCENE 2

To open:	Atmospheric lighting: coloured lanterns are lit and candles on kitchen shelf and on the trophy card table	
Cue 25	**Bridget**: "...why I'm going to Listowel." *Slowly focus on* **Bridget** *and* **Maureen**	(Page 67)
Cue 26	**Bridget**: "It's been a long time." *Return lighting to its previous level*	(Page 68)
Cue 27	**Margaret** turns off lantern lights *Turn off lantern lights*	(Page 71)
Cue 28	**Margaret** and **Bridget** exit *Fade to spotlight on* **Jamie**	(Page 71)
Cue 29	After **Jamie** pauses *Bring up light on* **Bridget**	(Page 71)
Cue 30	**Jamie**: "...really close in the last months." *Fade light out on* **Bridget** *and* **Maureen**	(Page 71)
Cue 31	**Jamie**: "The guest house is flourishing." *Bring up light on* **Celia** *and* **Brendan**	(Page 71)
Cue 32	**Jamie**: "...do a thing like that?" *Fade light out on* **Celia** *and* **Brendan**	(Page 71)
Cue 33	**Jamie**: "...that's love for you." *Bring up light on* **Margaret**	(Page 71)
Cue 34	**Jamie**: "I haven't seen her for years." *Fade light on* **Margaret**	(Page 71)

Cue 35	**Jamie**: "They settled near Manchester." *Bring up light on* **Eily** *and* **Brendan**	(Page 72)
Cue 36	**Jamie**: "…she had left him and gone South." *Fade light on* **Eily** *and* **Brendan**	(Page 72)
Cue 37	**Jamie**: "…and then they split up." *Bring up light on* **Paul**	(Page 72)
Cue 38	**Jamie**: "Wish you were here, Paul." *Fade light on* **Paul**	(Page 72)
Cue 39	**Jamie**: "Hardly a success story!" *Bring up light on* **Sarah**	(Page 72)
Cue 40	**Jamie**: "…the story of my life!" *Fade light on* **Sarah**	(Page 72)
Cue 41	**Jamie**: "Bridget would like that." *Dim lighting on tableau of characters round supper table*	(Page 72)
Cue 42	**Jamie** *takes a final look at the room* *Slowly fade to black-out*	(Page 73)

EFFECTS PLOT

ACT I

Cue 1	To open *Piano accompaniment for* The Kerry Dance *with rain effect. Fade during* **Jamie**'*s speech*	(Page 1)
Cue 2	Lights come up on *Riders to the Sea* actors *Britten's* Moonlight	(Page 2)
Cue 3	**Cathleen** kneels *Fade music; applause for eight seconds*	(Page 2)
Cue 4	**Maureen**: "Miss Moorhouse is late." *Sound of cars leaving the car park*	(Page 15)
Cue 5	**Margaret**: "You too, Sarah." *Britten's* Moonlight *from record player*	(Page 22)
Cue 6	**Eily** turns off the music *Cut music*	(Page 22)
Cue 7	They look at their scripts *Music swells, Britten's* Storm; *perhaps with first two lines of Synge's play*	(Page 23)
Cue 8	To open Scene 2 *Raining effect*	(Page 23)

ACT II

Cue 9	**Paul** watches the technical rehearsal *Final lines of the play on speaker as script page 40*	(Page 40)
Cue 10	**Bridget**: "Enough's been said." *Car horn from the car park*	(Page 63)

Cue 11	**Eily**: "Magic? Oh, yes." *Car horn again*	(Page 63)
Cue 12	Light fades in on **Jamie** *Faintly play piano accompaniment for* The Kerry Dance	(Page 71)
Cue 13	Lights start to fade on tableau *Fade piano music*	(Page 73)

www.ingramcontent.com/pod-product-compliance
Ingram Content Group UK Ltd.
Pitfield, Milton Keynes, MK11 3LW, UK
UKHW021844210426
5322IPUK00022B/461